# The Pagan In Recovery

*The Twelve Steps From A*
*Pagan Perspective*

Deirdre A. Hebert

# The Pagan
# In Recovery
*Twelve Steps From A*
*Pagan Perspective*

Deirdre A. Hebert

Asphodel Press

Hubbardston, Massachusetts

**Asphodel Press**
12 Simond Hill Road
Hubbardston, MA 01452

The Pagan In Recovery: The Twelve Steps From
A Pagan Perspective
© 2011 by Deirdre A. Hebert
ISBN 978-0-9825798-6-2

Printed in cooperation with
Lulu Enterprises, Inc.
860 Aviation Parkway, Suite 300
Morrisville, NC 27560

# Acknowledgements

I owe a huge debt of gratitude to all those who helped me achieve sobriety in my own life. There were so many people who taught me that I was deserving of a life that is second to none, even when I couldn't believe it myself. I learned that I could be trusted, and trustworthy. I learned that I had something to offer. They believed in me when I couldn't. I know that I can't remember all of their names, but I especially want to thank Laura, Cathy, Rene, Steve, Bruce, Bob, Erica, Mary, Nancy, Randy, Pat and Rick.

A huge debt of gratitude is owed to Julia Passamonti-Colamartino, for years of encouragement, and especially for taking a rough sketch and turning it into the beautiful emblem on the cover of this book. She is a brilliant artist, and you can find more of her work at her web site: http://www.venetiancat.com.

I also owe a debt of gratitude to the artist's community at One Washington Center in Dover, NH where I have my studio. This amazing group of people continued to urge me on as I worked on this book. They gave me encouragement and support throughout the project. Many thanks to Amanda, Rebecca, Rachel, Aaron, Beth, Ann and all the rest of that marvelous community. Rebecca Proctor, in particular has been amazingly encouraging. She owns RSP Studio and framed the cover of this book for me. She can be found at http://rspstudiocustomframing.com/

Many thanks to Alix Joyal for taking my photograph for the back cover. Alix is a talented artist who creates amazing quilts. You can find her work at http://www.mamakamills.com.

Lastly, but certainly not least, I must thank the Pagan community in both the New Hampshire area and beyond. It's you who let me realize when I first had the idea to write this book, that it was truly needed. Again, there are a great many people to thank, and not enough space to do so. But chief among these are my teacher, Priscilla, and those who have supported this effort: Kitty, Meical, Julia, Dino, Dawn, Amanda, Fae and so many others.

I apologize to anyone I might have forgot to name specifically – this was merely the failing of a very human person.

# Contents

# Foreword

This book is a guide to the Twelve Steps for Pagans. It is not specific to any Twelve-Step program and is in no way designed to compete with or replace any of them. Rather, it is meant to be used in conjunction with whatever Twelve Step program that the reader is involved in. It may be used for retreats by those who are working such a program, or it may be used by those who do not have a problem with addiction, as a basis for a truly unique spiritual experience.

This book was written to fill what I see is a major void in Pagan literature. While there are a number of self-help books for Pagans – some even dealing with addiction and recovery (notably among these is The Recovery Spiral by Cynthia Jane Collins), I was not able to find a single book dealing with Twelve Step programs from a Pagan perspective. I feel this is a major omission and I hope that the current volume at least begins to fill that void.

To understand the language in this text, please note that I was trained as a Wiccan for a number of years, and have studied other forms of Paganism – some formally, others informally. I do not identify myself as adhering to any specific Pagan tradition, though my first teacher tends to think of me as much more a Druid than a Wiccan these days. The reason this is important is because it may help the reader understand my choice of words through the text. While some are looking for an explanation of the Twelve Steps that avoid Christian ideas, others may think that the text may be "too Wiccan" or that it may more suited to those who identify as nonspecific Neo-Pagan rather than Hellenics, Norse Heathens, or other more specific groups. I have tried to be inclusive, but this is a difficult task, and I suspect that no one reading this with a critical eye and seeking to have a particular spiritual path uniquely affirmed will come away completely satisfied. Please keep in mind that this book is not written with any single or particular Pagan view in mind.

The language in the text may include more Wiccan ideas than, say, Druid or Heathen or Thelemic – the truth is that there are more Wiccans in the world, but hopefully practitioners of other Pagan faiths will recognize the references and the meanings. My job as an author is to present this information to the widest audience possible, and references that are known to many are likely going to resonate with a wider group of people. At the same time, I have used references from a variety of sources, and it is my hope that in the understanding of each other, we may come together to help those of us in need of healing from addiction or other problems to work together and find the healing we seek.

In my own experience I have found the Twelve Steps to afford one of the most profound spiritual experiences of my life. It's been suggested that all forms of addiction have, at their root, some search for or yearning for a spiritual experience. Our first experience with a substance seems, for a moment, to offer a glimpse of that experience, but each attempt to repeat or rediscover that fleeting feeling via that substance or activity leaves us further frustrated. For some people, an obsessive tendency follows, and they are unable to let go or disentangle from that cycle of using, and an inevitable emotional let-down follows.

At times, this spiritual, physical and emotional disorder can take on such proportions that it leads to legal problems such as OUI charges, loss of driving privileges, or even jail time. It can result in suicide – or worse, the knowledge that while under the influence, we may have taken the life of another person, perhaps while driving and intoxicated. We may lose friends and family because our behavior becomes so erratic and unpredictable that they can no longer live with or even be around us. Whatever the progression of this disease, it leaves the afflicted alone and empty. It is at this point though, where a person is now able to seek in earnest that which will truly fulfill them.

In working through our problems with the Twelve Steps, we are engaged in a journey of self-discovery that quite strangely takes us toward what we were seeking when we first took up whatever substance or activity it is that we used. It's an irony that we find, emerging from the jungle of addiction, exactly what it was that led us into a dark and potentially deadly wilderness in the first place.

Deirdre A. Hebert
February, 2010

# Introduction

At the beginning, let me be clear: this book is not about an easy way to break the cycle of addiction. There is no simple spell which one can recite which will render one cured from an addiction to alcohol, smoking or any other substance or habit that has taken over our lives. Many people have the mistaken notion that magick is about reciting some simple incantation and somehow, mysteriously, what we hope for comes to pass. In fact, many spells can take days, months or even years to cast. After casting the spell, or rather after performing the ritual portion of the spell, work – and a great deal of it – may still be required. You'll find no easy answers between the covers of this book.

Recovery from addictions is a major work, and if we're going to cure it using magick, it will require an especially potent form of magick. I found that that this magick already exists, and it's in a program called the Twelve Steps. Some might argue with me that this program is not magick; I disagree. Aleister Crowley stated that Magick is the art and science of causing change in conformity with will. If this definition is true, then the program of recovery of the Twelve Steps is magick of the highest order, because it is able to effect change in our very wills, enabling us to regain mastery of them, rather than having them blown and tossed by the whims and caprice of our environments and those around us. Crowley further stated that "Every intentional act is a magickal act." (Crowley, *Thelema*) The Twelve Steps give us back our own intention – that part of our self which, wittingly or unwittingly, we had abandoned.

The Twelve Steps comprise a spiritual program that allow the practitioner to bring about sobriety and serenity in those who, previously finding neither, sought refuge in a bottle, a pill, a needle or virtually any other substance or habit which held out the slightest promise of bringing relief, or filling some unknown void which perpetually hounded them. Each of us who became addicted was blinded to the truth that we were looking for something which is unattainable unless we find it first in ourselves.

Ever since Bill W. and Dr. Bob penned the text of *Alcoholics Anonymous* and its companion, *Twelve Steps and Twelve Traditions*, alcoholics worldwide have been able to find relief from the paralyzing and ultimately terminal disease of alcoholism. They have found a way to break the destructive pattern the disease imposes, and to live their lives with renewed enthusiasm and vigor. They have found their character, their relationships and their spirituality restored. So successful has this program been that its principles were adopted for use by those with other crippling addictions including narcotics, pills, smoking, sex, gambling, eating disorders, and just about any other behavior that becomes compulsive. Success in these areas has been encouragement to attempt the use of these principles in areas beside addiction; people are successfully implementing the principles of the Twelve Steps for problems such as certain mental illnesses. While not affording a cure from chronic disorders, the steps enable those who suffer from such conditions as depression, bipolar disorder, borderline personality disorder, and other conditions, to live their lives more fully and successfully.

The heart of the Twelve Steps is a spiritual program that permits the individual – indeed, requires the individual – to develop a deeper connection to Deity; to "God as we understood him", as the book *Alcoholics Anonymous* words it. Bill W and Dr. Bob were Christians (although it's been documented that Bill W. did at least dabble or experiment in spiritualism and the occult), and the program they devised was heavily influenced by their Christianity. While the program is incredibly effective, the Christian language of the texts used by Alcoholics Anonymous and other Twelve Step programs can make them daunting for those who follow a religion which has historically been at odds with Christianity.

While many Pagans might recall the burning times, and the real animosity that some Christians and Pagans have toward each other, the differences lie far deeper than the mere antagonism that has existed between the two faith traditions. Perhaps the major stumbling blocks for the Pagan seeking relief through the Twelve Steps are the paradigmatic differences between Christianity and Paganism. Christianity views the world as separate from God, a mere creation of God. It views God as a single being who is distant from us, unknowable and incomprehensible. Paganism views Deity as deeply connected to the world; beings who can be approached by the lay person without the intervention of a special priestly class. Indeed, through drawing down or through other rituals, we can connect to deity on a deep and intimate level without the need for priests or ministers to speak to the Divine or our behalf, or to us on behalf of the Gods. In Paganism, we can all be in direct communion with deity.

These differences do not suggest or indicate a weakness in the spiritual program of the Twelve Steps when used by Pagans. Rather, they point to the fact that the world has changed dramatically in the past 75 years, and these texts weren't written to communicate this program to those who do not share the fundamental belief system of the Christian tradition – that is, to religions that most, then, did not even know existed. Those who are in the business of translating books or poetry from one language to another know that the translation process must be done on multiple levels. The first level is that of language, of simply stating the meanings of the various words, sentences and verses in another language – for example, to translate *maison rouge* in French to "red house" in English. But beyond the simple exchange of words or meanings is a second level of translation, a level of culture. The *maison rouge*, or red house, may today correspond to the Red Tent movement of women. People of different cultures may not only speak a different language, but will also view the world differently. They may interact with the world and with each other in a fashion that would not be understood by others. Such is the difference between Christians and Pagans. It's not merely a difference of one God vs. many, but a completely different way of relating to deity and to the world.

The power contained within the program of the Twelve Steps is undeniable, as the millions who have recovered from their various addictions will attest. Anyone who diligently and honestly works them will attain some form of recovery. The purpose of this text is not to change these steps, but to make them available to those who view them through the eyes of a Pagan. In this book we'll open up these steps and demonstrate that the spiritual principles contained within them transcend any single religious paradigm. We'll show that "God, as we understood him" was truly meant to be far more inclusive than even those who penned the words in the first place may have imagined. We'll show that the only barrier to achieving the miracles offered to the sick and suffering is their ability to understand the steps and to believe that they do apply to each of us, no matter what religious tradition we may follow. The reader will begin to recognize that anyone who is willing to look beyond the language of the original Twelve Steps can bridge the gaps of culture and language, and can achieve freedom from addiction and compulsive behavior.

These steps have worked such magick in people's lives that those who have achieved not only sobriety but an entirely new way of life through them have often wondered what the world would be like if everyone lived by these principles. I have heard ministers base sermons on the Twelve Steps, hoping that their congregations would embrace them. Some supervisors have tried to use the principles they contain in their workplace. I'm not sure though, that the Twelve Steps will gain widespread public acceptance ... they don't have the glitter of pop-psychology, and the average person is missing one thing that the addict, alcoholic and compulsive possesses: the addict, the alcoholic, and the compulsive are desperate. For the average person, a failure to achieve a spiritual awakening means nothing but a failure to achieve a spiritual awakening. For the addict, alcoholic, or compulsive, failure to overcome their addictions can literally mean the difference between life and death, or at least the difference between a pleasant or an intolerable life. For such as us, success is not an option; it's not marked by merely feeling better after trying some techniques we discover in a workbook. Rather, quite literally, it means that we may live to tell the tale instead of being found dead behind a dumpster. Those of us who survive, who achieve the sobriety and the way of life promised in these steps have also the unfortunate duty of bidding farewell to those who don't make it. It is my sincere hope that you who read this book and practice the principles in it are among those who survive.

# The Twelve Steps

The Twelve Steps, in their original form from the book *Alcoholics Anonymous*, are outlined in Chapter 5. They are the essence of what is contained in the first 164 pages of that same book. The remaining pages of the text of *Alcoholics Anonymous* contain personal stories chosen to be representative of those who suffer from alcoholism in order to demonstrate to those contemplating the need for such a program in their lives what a "real alcoholic" looks like.

With the success of the program, Dr. Bob and Bill W. created a second text book called Twelve Steps and Twelve Traditions. The first part of this book showed the individuals who chose to work through these steps exactly how to do so. Combined with the book *Alcoholics Anonymous*, anyone who needed it had access to a complete program of recovery from alcoholism. It was these two books which paved the way for all the other Twelve Step based programs of recovery that have become popular over the years. Even early on, the success of this program was noteworthy and inspiring. Wives, physicians and clergy would send previously helpless cases to Alcoholics Anonymous because it had helped so many others. Soon it was realized that it wasn't only the low-bottom, hopeless, alcoholic man in need of this help, and many wives, physicians and clergy soon joined the ranks of those whose lives were saved by this program of recovery. It was discovered that long before the alcoholic reached the streets and the gutters, their problem was evident, and people began seeking help long before things got that bad. Then the program spread to other problems, and the Twelve Steps are now virtually everywhere.

The Twelve Steps accomplish a number of goals that are important to any Pagan practitioner:

**1. They are a system for gaining or increasing self-knowledge.** We're all familiar with the words of the Oracle at Delphi: Know Thyself. We're equally familiar with the words of Socrates who said "The unexamined life is not worth living." Those who do not engage in a process of self examination will never learn from their mistakes. Such people are little more than automatons or animals running on instinct alone. However good and sincere their hearts, they cannot learn or grow to a degree which leads to true empowerment. It is the process of self-appraisal that permits us to understand how what we've done will affect us in the future. It permits us to look ahead when making a decision, and with some accuracy, to determine if that action is indeed worth the consequences. It helps us understand our reasons, our motivation, our true and highest will.

**2. They are a code of conduct.** As Pagans, we know that we are responsible for our actions. We have no God to whom we must go for absolution of sins, no being who will wash us clean of our misdeeds. The saying "It's better to do what you want and then ask forgiveness later" simply doesn't apply in the Pagan world. All accounts must be settled. The Twelve Steps teach us to make amends for our wrongs, to stand up and take responsibility, whatever the consequences, for what we've done and offer us a system to do so.

**3. They teach us that with faith, we're far stronger than we would be without it.** They show us that faith isn't so much a crutch as it is a walking stick. It is a tool which may not be needed all the time, but it certainly makes things easier when we have it. And when we do need it, it's right at hand. A crutch implies a broken person. A walking stick implies one who is not afraid of adventure. A crutch imposes, by its nature, limitations upon that broken individual. When we need crutches, we don't climb mountains or go on long hikes in the wilderness. On the other hand, with a walking stick in our hand, we are telling the world that we are ready to experience the new and the wonderful.

**4. They teach us that helping others is paramount to our survival.** In giving, we also receive. There is an old saying that goes "You can't have your cake and eat it too." One might also believe that you can't have what you've got and give it away too. But strangely, this is not true. The truth is that to keep what you've got, you must give it away. As Pagans, we're often fond of the paradox, and this is one of the truest of paradoxes. To keep our own sobriety, we must offer it to others. To maintain our sanity, we must show others the way to achieve it as well.

The Twelve Steps must be taken in the order presented. They simply will not work otherwise. In Step 1, we admit that we have a problem. If we never make such an admission, what is the point of the following eleven? In Step 7, we ask our higher power to remove or transform our shortcomings. If we don't know what they are (Step 4), how will we know what to ask for? Furthermore, how will we know if there is any success? In Step 9, we seek to make amends with those we have harmed. Without a careful survey of those we might have harmed (Step 8), how will we know to whom we must make such amends?

Few programs devised by men or women have been both so carefully thought out and yet so simple to perform. Usually we meddle and tweak and hack and staple and cut and paste until we've created some behemoth that more resembles a bill in the American Congress. It may have thousands of pages, and not a single person will have read its entirety. Or it might resemble a pre-flight checklist, where one may be insured a safe take-off, but there is no supporting documentation to explain why each step is necessary.

Unlike many other successful and important works, the documentation provided with the Twelve Steps is thorough but not overly verbose. It tells us "precisely how we have recovered" (*Alcoholics Anonymous* – Foreword to the First Edition) without being a daunting tome that only a professional can understand. It's not simplistic like many of those "self-help" books, nor is it based on pop psychology or fad science. It is simply a step-by-step description of how the first few people who got together managed to solve a problem that had been perplexing them and their physicians for many years: how could they get sober, and having gotten sober, how could they remain so?

In the following pages, we'll take a look at each of these steps. We'll examine them from a Pagan perspective and see exactly how they can help anyone who suffers from addiction, including us as Pagans. We'll avoid monotheistic or specifically Christian language except to point out that the original authors truly intended to make these steps available to everyone. The steps, as we use them in this book are as follows:

## The Twelve Steps

**Step 1:**
Admitted that we were powerless, and that our lives had become unmanageable.

**Step 2:**
Came to believe that a power greater than ourselves could restore us to sanity.

**Step 3:**
Made a decision to turn our will and our lives over to the care of the Divine and our own highest self.

**Step 4:**
Made a searching and fearless moral inventory of ourselves.

**Step 5:**
Admitted to Deity, to ourselves, and to another human being the exact nature of our wrongs.

**Step 6:**
Were entirely ready to have the Divine transform all these defects of character.

**Step 7:**
Humbly asked the Divine to transform us.

**Step 8:**
Made a list of all persons we had harmed, and became willing to make amends to them all.

**Step 9:**
Made direct amends to such people wherever possible, except when to do so would bring harm to them or others.

**Step 10:**
Continued to take personal inventory, and when we were wrong, promptly admitted it.

**Step 11:**
Sought through prayer, meditation and our craft to improve our conscious contact with Deity, praying for knowledge and understanding of our own highest will, the Divine plan, and the power to carry that out.

**Step 12:**
Having had a spiritual awakening as the result of these steps, we tried to carry this message to others, and to live these principles in all our affairs.

In this text, I may include a number of personal examples and anecdotes, mostly from my own experience, to show that anyone with a sincere desire to achieve and maintain sobriety through the use of these steps should be able to do so. The text of *Alcoholics Anonymous* contains about 400 pages of personal stories, which enable the reader to identify with the issues that caused so many others to seek relief from alcoholism. Personal anecdotes from a Pagan in recovery may help other Pagans to recognize exactly how this program can be of help to them.

Many Pagans are used to performing acts of magic. The Twelve Steps are something of an alchemical program, a work designed to transform our very lives. With any magical work, energy must be raised and directed. The practitioner must be fearless, diligent, steadfast, and dedicated to the work. Anything less might result in failure. For the alchemist or the ceremonialist, failure can result in disaster. For the addict or alcoholic, failure often leads to a few possible outcomes ... jails, institutions or death. Recovery is a daunting journey and failure affords dire consequences. Today, at least in the United States, institutions are fewer than they were a century ago, so we can add a fourth terminus for the addict ... the streets. For a time, I was among the homeless, and I've known many who live on the streets. One whom I knew was found dead behind a dumpster, another at a riverside, another alone in an apartment. This is not how our journeys into the West were meant to be taken. If we work these steps diligently, we'll live to take our final journey with boldness and dignity.

Each step presented in this work consists of three major sections. In the first section, we try to understand the meaning of the step, its purpose and the principles behind it from a Pagan perspective. This will give us an intellectual knowledge of the step. In the second part, we look at the practical application of the step in our daily lives. In the third part, we have a ritual that is designed either to prepare us to perform that step as we are working through them in our own program of recovery, or to actually accomplish that step. Some of these steps are undeniably daunting, and at times, some sort of preparation can help. You may use these rituals as written, or, if you wish, you can modify them for your own purpose. The point, the goal, is to offer real and tangible experiences as the steps are completed.

# Step 1

## *Admitted that we were powerless, and that our lives had become unmanageable.*

### The Foundation

This is the foundational step of the entire Twelve Step program of recovery. Unless this step is accomplished, nothing that is done afterward has much if any chance of success. It is also the most difficult step to take, for as soon as we take it we have acknowledged powerlessness and a lack of control – two things which no one, seemingly, in their right mind would wish to do. Why is it so crucial that we acknowledge that we are powerless and out of control? Why is it that we must admit that we have hit bottom? Why must we admit defeat prior to having any hope of victory? This last question sounds almost self-contradictory. Fortunately for us, nothing is farther from the truth.

The reason for all of this, for admitting powerlessness and a lack of control, for hitting our bottom, and for admitting defeat is simply because unless we do these things, we have no need for recovery. One doesn't take insulin or chemotherapy until one recognizes that they are diabetic or that they have cancer. Nobody goes through a difficult and potentially painful form of therapy unless they are first convinced that they have an illness that requires these things. Until we are able to admit defeat, we may well be under some illusion that we are still in control, that by some act of sheer willpower, we might yet accomplish that which we've already proved unable to do.

As Pagans, we don't tend to view power as something that is separate from us; we tend to know that we can find all the power we need within us. This is a philosophy that is somewhat implicit in the *Charge of the Goddess*. Doreen Valiente wrote: "... if that which thou seekest, thou findest not within thee, thou wilt never find it without." How can it be that the power of deity resides within us, yet we still remain powerless? The truth is, though, that this is only an apparent paradox. We are powerless, not because we are without power or ability, but because we have lost the means to put the power within us to use. We are like the automobile with a powerful engine which no longer has a working transmission. While that engine runs beautifully, it has no way to transmit the energy, the motivating force, to the wheels. Likewise, in us, the power remains, but it is unusable because we have, wittingly or not, abandoned the ability to access or utilize that power. Deity has not abandoned us; we've simply lost touch with the divine within us.

### What is meant by "unmanageable"?

As for our lives becoming unmanageable, we need to come to terms with this as well. This is likely as distasteful a term as powerlessness. We may still be able to get to work each day – many of us have high-paying jobs. How then, can we come to the admission that our lives are unmanageable? What constitutes "unmanageable"?

We may well have that high-paying job – but is there a chance that whatever habit we have is keeping us from performing even better, and thus preventing us from a promotion that we might have otherwise attained? Our family life might not seem to be suffering, but have we ever missed a sporting event that one of our children wished us to see, simply because we were sporting a hangover? We might think we're responsible, but does our partner really trust us as they once did? The truth is that like an infection, despite the fact that things appear manageable right now, they're not going to get better unless we recognize the problem and take action. Like an infection, the disease of addiction is out of control the moment we have it – it is progressive and will have its way.

At the other end of the scale, things may still seem quite manageable to us – we, as human beings, have a unique ability to hide the truth from our selves. That same truth though, will likely be quite visible to those around us. We may not have an address, but we seemingly have freedom. We may not have a job, but nobody is telling us what to do. We may have lost our license, but we can still get around quite well, using bicycles, walking or with public transportation. We might say that "we're helping the environment" when the truth is that we simply have no choice. Surely our drug deals provide us with enough left over to satisfy ourselves. If things get really out of hand, we know a few people who have some drugs that they certainly won't miss. As we go down the scale, as the bottoms get deeper, we recognize that the stores make lots of money ... they won't miss what we can slip in our pockets. If things get really desperate, who cares if we rob a store or snatch a purse? Certainly we're managing our situations! Somehow, the lower we go, the better we are at rationalizing our situation.

The truth is that none of this is freedom. Freedom is not simply about not being locked up somewhere; it's not about being in possession of the keys to the buildings we are currently housed in. Freedom is about being able to make our own choices. When our lives are unmanageable, we are no longer making our own choices. We're pretending – we're trying to fool ourselves because it makes our situation more tolerable. When we're homeless, for most of us who are addicts or alcoholics or compulsives, that isn't a choice. It's because we've been kicked out of the last place where we lived, unwelcome to live with those who may still be our friends, but can't bear to watch what we're doing with our lives. Homelessness isn't freedom; it's something that is a direct result of not being in control of our own lives.

At the time that I'm writing this, joblessness is at a near record high. But there is a qualitative difference between the merely unemployed and the unemployed alcoholic or addict. The job market is turning around, and for the "merely unemployed", there may be a light at the end of the tunnel. They may be retraining for other positions as they become available, they may be touching up their resumes. But for many alcoholics and addicts, a "job" consists of something that will provide enough money to purchase the next bottle or hit. The light at the end of the tunnel doesn't exist because they may quite simply not even be able to recognize that they exist within a tunnel. Some of those who are addicted aren't even looking for that light. We remain in a constant state of denial that tells us that nothing is really wrong, and if anything is, well, it is certainly someone else's fault, and not up to us at all to fix. The tunnel we're in seems safe, and we don't want to leave. But this tunnel doesn't have room for both us and the train that's on its way down the tracks.

As we progress down the scale, we might find ourselves committing crimes in order to survive. We become filled with resentment toward anyone who has more than us. The mere fact that someone "has" while we "have not" is cause enough for us to become angry. The cause becomes unimportant ... they "have", we "need", so we take. Not all of us descend to the depths where we will consciously steal the possessions of another, but in our addictions, few of us have not done so on at least an unconscious level. Many of us who might be professional sorts have padded expense accounts to pay our drinking or sex or drug habits. Many of us have lied to spouses about where money seems to disappear to. Many of us have been inefficient at work, or outright drunk or stoned while on the job, perhaps we called in sick, when we were really hung-over or partying. All of this is a form of stealing.

It's interesting how many of us have said "this far, no farther", but then broken that promise. Young, we'll say "I'll never steal", but we hide what we're spending, then we borrow but forget to repay. Perhaps we'll overextend ourselves with our credit cards. Then we write a check that bounces. Each of these steps leads just a bit further to outright robbery.

This behavior is mirrored in our abuse of substances. We might start out drinking beer or smoking pot. We say that we'll stay away from the "hard stuff". But perhaps the disease progresses. The next step on the ladder is never that far away. Having had our share of beer, wine doesn't seem that bad. Drinking wine, brandy doesn't seem that bad. Drinking brandy, whiskey is acceptable. Smoking pot – what's hash but strong pot? Using hash regularly, perhaps cocaine isn't that bad. If we snort coke, snorting heroin mustn't be that bad.

Sooner or later, we find that the lines we said we would never cross are far behind us. None of us, when we were young, would ever admit that we would one day find ourselves throwing up in a public park because we were drunk. None of us would have ever dreamed that we would find ourselves with a needle in our arm. None of us would have imagined that we would so pollute our bodies with substances that others would need to take care of us because we were no longer able to stand or walk under our own power, that our livers would be visible through our distended bellies, or that we would now walk around with yellow eyes and skin and rotting teeth.

One of the questions that I've been asked by some is "How do I know that my life is unmanageable?" Not everyone has shot up. Not everyone has had an OUI or lost their license. Not everyone has been put in protective custody. So how can one know without ambiguity that yes, indeed, a life is unmanageable? There have been multiple self-help tests produced. Most of them have some questions in common. Here is a list of questions to ponder:

> ➢ Have you ever put someone else's life in danger because you were using substances? (Think before you answer this question. Have you ever got behind the wheel of a car knowing you were buzzed or high?)
> ➢ Have you ever placed your employment or education in jeopardy because of your use of substances?
> ➢ Have you ever endangered your relationships because of your use of substances?
> ➢ Have others been concerned about your use of substances and brought it to your attention?
> ➢ Have you ever endangered your own health with substance abuse?

➢ Have you ever found yourself in situations you would not have placed yourself in had you been sober?

➢ Have you ever blacked out when using substances (lost time, found yourself waking in strange places, had people tell you things you were involved in, but have no recollection of doing so)?

➢ Have you found yourself unable to resist "just one more"?

➢ Have you found yourself using more than you intended?

➢ Has your use of substances interfered with your ability to meet your financial obligations?

➢ Have you missed important family, social or work events because of your substance use?

➢ Have you ever lost a place to live as a result of your substance use?

If you can answer no to all of these questions, truthfully, then perhaps you don't have a problem. But if you've answered "yes" to any of these, then there is a good chance that looking into the situation further will be of real benefit to you. This doesn't mean that you are an alcoholic or an addict – but it's worth checking out.

There is something interesting about recognizing that one is somehow out of control. It only takes one chink in the armor, and soon one finds that the level of control that we thought we had in our lives was only illusory. When I first admitted that my life was unmanageable, I had no OUI hanging over my head, I hadn't lost a job as a result of substance abuse. I was certain that I could answer each of the above questions in the negative. I was seeing a therapist for an unrelated problem, and I thought she had quite a bit of gall to suggest that I might have a problem. How dare she?

But some time passed, and I pondered her suggestion. I went to a meeting and met people who I believed were far worse off than I. I was feeling quite good about my situation and left. A few months later, after a binge and an overdose, I awoke in intensive care. I had been restrained because I was combative. My stomach had been pumped, I had a catheter because I couldn't control my bladder. I had been picked up by a friend, walking in the middle of a major thoroughfare, disrupting traffic, and unaware of what I was doing. It was only after this incident that I admitted to myself that I had a real problem; that my life was unmanageable.

After making this admission, and after some time working these steps, I began to realize that my level of control and my ability to manage my own life was far less than what I had imagined. I found that contrary to what I had first thought, I could answer "yes" to nearly every question listed above. While I never got an

OUI, I certainly drove while high or intoxicated; I had certainly endangered the lives of others. (I recall one perplexing morning when I was removing leaves and branches from the side of my car, wondering how they had got there.) I had never lost a job because of drinking or using, but after the company which I had last worked for failed, I didn't get another job. I "thought" I had never damaged any relationships because of my substance use, but my oldest daughter refused to speak with me for a number of years because I was "crazy". I thought I had never been homeless, but my friend's mother's couch was by no means an address. The point is that if we can honestly answer in the affirmative to any of these questions, it's quite likely that we've already gone much farther down the scale than we have the immediate ability to see for ourselves. If others are mentioning to us that we might have a problem, the chance is that we do have a problem.

I'm not suggesting at this stage that everyone who reads this should jump up and say "I'm Jane (or John or Sue or David) and I'm an addict or an alcoholic." But certainly, if you've got this book in your hand and you're not reading it for professional reasons, there's a good chance that you or someone close to you might benefit from a good dose of introspection, and perhaps from attending a Twelve Step meeting and asking someone how one can know if they really need such a program.

## Surrender

Some call this admission of powerlessness and the recognition that our lives are unmanageable a surrender. Surrender is another word that has a negative connotation to many. We are brought up in a world where "retreat" and "surrender" imply defeat and weakness. We are taught that with the power of the will, we ought to be able to overcome our natures, and that only those who are weak or lacking in fortitude and morals would ever become addicted to a substance. People of good character simply don't find themselves in such a situation. Certainly while there have been a few prominent individuals who have been hospitalized because of addictions, these are rare cases, and may be the result of the combination of too much time on their hands along with too much money. It's somewhat expected among rock stars, and certainly they'll quit when they get older.

In our society, heavily influenced with Christian asceticism as it is and with so many churches still preaching temperance, becoming addicted is viewed as a moral issue. Whether we wish to admit it or not, we've likely been influenced with these views as well. Often we tend to believe that if anything is in control of us, then we are morally deficient. We seek to gain control over that which has us in its grip. We seek to break free from these talons with our own will-power. Many of us, as Pagans, will try to work magic or seek divine assistance through prayer, or to look for the answer in runes or the Tarot. In each of these cases though, we're looking in the wrong place simply because we are seeking a way to control that which is ultimately beyond our control.

In the case of addiction, surrender doesn't imply that one surrenders to the disease. Rather it is a surrender to the fact that we have a problem. We surrender in the sense that we recognize that there is no power which we can possibly muster under our own efforts that will solve this problem. We surrender because we recognize that in this situation, we are truly powerless. But in this surrender resides a miracle, and as we work through the remaining steps, that miracle will become more and more apparent. At the moment, we feel beaten, but this needs to happen because it is our starting point. It is the first clear marker or solid foothold that we've had, quite likely, in a number of years. Up to this point, we've been adrift in a small boat in the vast sea that has been our affliction. Now, in our surrender, we've stuck a white flag in the soil in the first island we found in this sea. We've said, possibly with great trepidation, "I'm an addict or alcoholic (or whatever words it may be that we use), and I need help." Our knees may be shaking, our head may not be held very high at all, but the words come out of our mouths, and that flag is planted. No matter where the path takes us now, we have one familiar place from which we can now find our way and measure our progress. Now we can take a bearing and begin the journey. We may not see the light at the end of the tunnel, but we know now that there is a tunnel, and unlike the dangerous one we were in, this one at least has room enough so that when, and if that train passes, we won't be hit by it.

Most everyone who has taken this step will remember the first time they uttered those words. Some will remember where they were, who was with them, and quite possibly the very date. As confused as we may be at this point in our lives, the first time we say "I am an alcoholic" or "I am an addict" is a memorable occasion. It is so because it likely represents the first time, in a long time, that we have been entirely honest with ourselves.

### Morality

One more word that must be spoken of when we regard the problem of addiction is morality. The truth is that addiction and compulsion have little to do with morality. So many people find themselves in a state of self-condemnation because they feel that they are addicted because of some sort of moral weakness or deficiency of character, and that's simply not the case. Being an alcoholic or an addict says *nothing* about your character. It doesn't mean you're weak, it doesn't mean you're committing some sort of sin – it means simply that your body reacts to these substances or compulsions in a way in which others do not. Most all of us have tried to overcome our obsessions and compulsions and have found that we were unable to do so. The problem isn't a lack of will, but a lack of power over our illness. The Twelve Steps will lead us to the source of that power.

Now this does not excuse any of our *actions* while we were under the influence of whatever substance you might have used. Nor does this excuse our behavior between binges. We are, each one of us, responsible for each of our actions, and these may have some moral implications, but being an addict or an alcoholic is not a choice – it's a biological process that we do not have control over. None of us ever took that first drink, or first hit and said "I really want to be an addict." We cannot engage in this process while we harbor the feeling that we are somehow morally deficient simply because some substance has a grip on us. There will be plenty enough in our lives that we will need to take responsibility for; let's not begin by hoisting upon our shoulders some weight we need not bear.

# Step 1 Practical Application

Maybe you're in therapy and your therapist has suggested that you might want to look at your relationship with drugs or alcohol; perhaps a school counselor or family member has suggested that you have a problem. Maybe it's gone on so long that your job or education is in jeopardy. You might have found yourself in jail or before a judge who is ordering you to a treatment program.

Everyone who has become addicted to a substance has found themselves at a low point – a bottom. The truth about bottoms is that they can all go deeper – all we need do is keep digging. Until we stop doing what we've been doing, that hole just gets deeper and more difficult to crawl out of.

Step 1 is only a recognition that we have hit some sort of bottom or other. We can't fix what we refuse to acknowledge as broken; it would be silly to bring a car that is in perfect order to our mechanic and ask him to fix it. It's just as silly, and much more dangerous, to drive around with a vehicle that has flat tires.

If we are in need of recovery and trying to live life without it, we are in the position of that driver behind the wheel of a defective car. It's up to us at this point to recognize that the car is in fact not drivable and that we steer or stop with difficulty. If we don't acknowledge the need for something to be done, there is little limit to the wreckage we might leave in our wake.

We might have already caused a great deal of damage to our selves, and to those around us. Here, in Step 1, we merely recognize that the wreckage is there. This isn't the time to make promises to those around us that "we're in a program now, and things will change". Instead of making more promises, such as those we've made before and broken, we will recognize that we are going to change who we are, and let that change speak for us.

Step 1, in which we discover our brokenness, is where we also find our hope.

## Step 1 Ritual

When many people think of ritual, they think of the elaborate ceremonies of Catholicism or of the complicated and dangerous rites of ceremonial magicians or the celebrations of Wiccans in their circles. Ritual doesn't need to be that elaborate or complex. In fact, the simplest acts that we do, so long as they are done thoughtfully, can be our rituals. A number of the rituals in this book will be of just that sort.

Each step in this process will be accompanied with a ritual. These are each rites of passage, and as the road to recovery is a true journey, these rituals are our way-markers. They are learning experiences and celebrations of our achievements.

Our first ritual in our path toward recovery helps us to acknowledge our helplessness and inability to control what is out of our hands. Our culture teaches us that we are or should be always in control and that there is nothing that we can't change by exercise of technology or will. While this is partly true, even technology has its challenges. Dams break, nuclear power plants melt down, our machines rust and fail ... everything that we have built, should humans leave this planet, will someday return to a natural state, and a million years from now, there will likely be little evidence that we ever existed.

Our first ritual takes place at a natural place where we can be in contact with the elements. It may be a stream or a shallow river. It might be the ocean or a mountaintop. Wherever it is, it must be as natural as possible, and we must come in contact with the elements of Earth. A rainstorm or snowstorm is good as well.

When you have found your place, stand in that space. If it's a stream or river or the ocean, stand in the water. If it's a mountain, stand on the top in the wind. If it's rain or snow, stand where you experience these on your body.

Now is the difficult part. Will nature to stop what it is doing. If you are in that stream or ocean, cause the water to stop its advance. On the hill or in the midst of the storm, use your will to stop the wind or rain. Obviously, this is not something that our will alone can control. Don't just intellectually understand this – experience it. (Some people are said to be able to control the weather by their will, but such people are not commonplace, and people who are so advanced are also likely to have far better control of their lives than most of us.) So stand there for a time and will the Earth to change. Do so until you recognize that the powers of the Earth are not at your command – at least at this moment. Such also is the case with addiction. It's not something we can will away. It is a power over us, just as is the power of the ocean. But like the ocean and the river and the stream and the mountaintop, all is in a state of change and transformation. All follows natural laws. Everything is becoming something new. For us there is a way out – a way from who and what we are, and toward that which we wish to become. We just haven't found it yet.

Now step out of that ocean or stream or come down from the mountain. Recognize that what we need for a safe journey is a guide. We are now on our way to Step 2, in which we are likely to meet that guide.

# Step 2

## *Came to believe that a power greater than ourselves could restore us to sanity.*

Having taken the first step, we are now ready to begin on our journey. Step 2, "Came to believe that a power greater than ourselves could restore us to sanity", marks the first minefield for the Pagan in recovery. This "power greater than ourselves" in most of the Western world is recognized as the Christian God. It's quite likely that a Pagan attending a Twelve Step meeting will be the only pagan there. Even the agnostic or the atheist attending such a meeting will have a good many Christian attitudes; they are unavoidable in the Western world. Those of us who left a Christian faith for a Pagan one might even still carry much of that baggage with us yet. Most Twelve Step meetings in the Western World either begin or end with the Lord's Prayer. Many an atheist, agnostic and Pagan have been put off the moment they hear "Our Father, who art in heaven". At these few words, many are turned off immediately. Some never return. Some die. This is not hyperbole.

Please don't get the impression that I'm blaming Christianity for more Pagan, atheist or agnostic deaths; I'm not. It's just a simple fact that we live in a world that is largely Christian, and that most of the people that we'll meet in the Twelve Step programs are also Christian. As a spiritual program, each member of the group will likely express their own religious beliefs. As groups, the opening and closing words will be voted on by those groups, and, in a democratic organization, the wishes of the larger group will likely prevail. There is no way around it ... if you attend meetings regularly, you'll hear religious speech. But in this comes another moment of freedom for the Pagan in recovery.

Where is this second moment of freedom? It comes from the knowledge that the Twelve Steps were never intended to be a religious program. This "power greater than ourselves" is only the Christian God to Christians. To others, it may be God and Goddess, Maiden, Mother and Crone, Great Spirit or anyone else. When we hear the Christians recite the Lord's Prayer, we can recognize that this is only one group of believers who are free to offer a prayer to their God. We, who believe differently, are quite able to do the same.

I remember early on being quite put off by the Christian prayer. Often, I would recite a prayer to the Mother, and I would do so in French. People would hear me praying, but in another language. I simply told them that I was reciting the prayer as I had learned it when I was young. I didn't tell them that I had replaced "Father" with "Mother". Most were simply happy to know that I was praying to *someone*, and the rest assumed that it was to the same god. But in Step 2, it isn't the object of our belief that is the most important issue. At this stage of our recovery, the real issue is *belief*.

## Belief

In Step 1, we admitted to ourselves that we were powerless, that our lives have become unmanageable. This leaves us with a great void, and it is imperative that this void be filled with something of substance. Lives left unmanageable and without power might quickly give way to hopelessness and desperation. Step 2 calls us to recognize that there truly is hope. It suggests to us that where we have found ourselves without power, or without access within ourselves to that power, that certainly we can look beyond ourselves.

As Pagans, most of us are quite fond of circles. We know that no matter where we are on a circle, so long as we keep moving in the same direction we will return to the beginning. Likewise, any search that takes us outside of ourselves, if conducted thoroughly enough, will lead us back within ourselves. Thus, where the Charge of the Goddess says "If that which thou seekest, thou findest not within thee" it doesn't necessarily suggest that we're not to look outside of ourselves. Rather, in looking anywhere, we will certainly find insight into our deeper selves. I believe that we're called to discover more about ourselves, no matter where we seek. As Pagans, we're called to recognize divinity within ourselves as well as without. At an early point in our recovery, what remains within us is in turmoil. Like a windswept lake, the surface is too rough to provide a clear vision of what lies below. But we are able at this point to look outward rather than inward, and this is what we need to do.

The Gods and Goddesses are of such a nature that if we seek them, we will eventually find them, and the seeking will eventually lead us right back to ourselves. But at this stage in our recovery, most of us are unable to look that deeply within us. We've likely left such a trail of wreckage and carnage that looking deeply may drive us right back to where we were. It's far easier to look beyond us, and that's all that's required at this stage. For many, this is a great mercy.

As Pagans, we have a great variety of places to look for a being that can restore us to sanity. We have Brighid who can heal. We have Kwan Yin, the Chinese Goddess of compassion, or Beiwe the Saami Goddess of sanity. We could call on almost any deity that we know, knowing that the gods and goddesses of nature seek to provide balance in nature. Addiction is an imbalance; it is the result of our instincts gone awry. Who better than the deities of nature to help us to restore them to their proper purpose and focus?

The Twelve Steps do not require that we believe in any particular being. In many meetings, you'll hear people speak of a higher power, and call that higher power Jesus or God (as if God is a proper name rather than a title), but it's vital as Pagans to know that the program does *not* require that we give any sort of recognition to someone else's god. Our trust must be in the god of our own understanding.

### Finding Belief Within Us

Many who enter a Twelve Step program hit a wall at belief. We have tried prayer, church, religion, self-help books, psychotherapy, hypnosis, in-patient and outpatient hospitalizations, rehabs, and almost any manner of relief imaginable, all to little or no effect. We've tried every system out there, still to come back to the same position we were at before. Many of us believe that we are special cases, those for whom no program will work.

Here is a secret: If you are capable of reading and understanding these words, you are capable of finding relief from addiction. There are few requirements that are necessary to find recovery, and I'll list them here:

1. You must be alive.
2. You must be capable of being honest with yourself.
3. You must have a functioning brain.

With these three tools, just about anyone should be capable of working through a program of recovery. If you possess the above capacities, the only things that are preventing you from finding recovery are your own lies and prejudices.

I was once outside and I noticed that my neighbor was on her hands and knees searching through the grass. I asked her what the matter was, and she told me that she had lost a ring. She asked me if I would help her find it. We searched and searched for close to an hour, and we simply couldn't find her ring. At this point she told me "It's lost. Let's just go inside and forget it." I remember

telling her at this point that the surest way to *not* find the ring
would be to stop looking, and I intended on looking a while longer.
It was getting darker, so I went into the house and got a flashlight.
I started, in a pattern, shining my light line by line across the grass
where she thought she had lost the ring, and, sure enough, I saw a
shimmer of gold under the light. She got her ring back.

The surest way to fail at recovery is to stop trying, to assume
that we are that one case who is beyond hope. Failure, like anything
else, is a choice. The hope, the good news, the silver lining in all
this is that as much as failure is a choice, so is success. Most who
fail at recovery simply don't want it bad enough. It's true that we
can't recover on our own; the book Alcoholics Anonymous says
rightly "without help, it is too much for us". The corollary to that is
that with help, we can succeed. We have those on our side who are
willing to help.

Many who call themselves Pagans have never truly sought a
relationship with Deity. This is your chance! Each of us is capable
of choosing to believe; we may not know in an intellectual or
empirical fashion, but we can believe. Whomever you choose to
follow as god or goddess, Step 2 is the moment when we trust in
faith that Deity is there and wishes to work on our side. "We came
to believe that a power greater than ourselves could restore us to
sanity." This doesn't mean that we get discouraged when we find
that we don't have all our marbles back right now. We are
embarking on a journey that will last quite a while ... we don't reach
the destination just a few hours out of port.

What we are given for a gift right away is hope. We are graced
with the knowledge that while we couldn't do this alone, we now
have an ally, or allies. Those who know us best will be our guides,
our cut-men at the corner as we wage battle with the obsession that
has tyrannized us. Our allies will guide us, dress our wounds when
we misstep, lift us up when we fall, and encourage us along the way.
All that is required of us is that bit of faith, trust and belief, along
with the willingness to work the steps and not give up when the
going gets difficult.

Right now, our job is not to worry about how we are going to
remain clean and sober for the rest of our lives; it's simply to
believe that where we may have experienced repeated failures,
we're no longer alone. Our job is to surrender to our allies rather
than our adversaries, to place our trust solely in those who have
our best interests in mind. Our task is to believe that our gods will
sustain us and restore our instincts to their proper place and
purpose. Our gods and goddesses stand before us at this very
moment, with hands reaching out for us, and ask simply "Are you

ready?" "Will you trust me?" If we can believe that a power greater than ourselves can restore us to sanity, then we are ready to move on to Step 3.

## Step 2 Practical Application

Believing that someone else believes something is a giant step away from believing something for ourselves. Many of us who have attended Twelve Step meetings have heard "you may not believe, but just for now, believe that we believe". That's a step, but it falls somewhat into the "wait and see" category of things. And when it's coming from an individual who believes something entirely different than we suspect to be true, it might not be a fulfilling proposition.

To "…come to believe that a power greater than us can restore us to sanity" implies not merely a suspicion, but a knowledge of some sort. The problem is that most people today associate knowledge with proof. We look to the word "knowledge" in the same sense as a scientist and an engineer, and expect the word to mean the same thing when used by a person of faith. This problem is further exacerbated by people of faith who claim to mean the same thing as the scientist when they use the word "knowledge".

When we seek recovery from addiction and are presented with Step 2, how can we reconcile the phrase "came to believe" with an intellect that tells us that we cannot believe that for which we have no proof? The answer lies in recognizing the sorts of proof that are available for various propositions. Of course, we have no instruments of scientific design that are capable of measuring and demonstrating the existence of God. Nor do we have any instruments that can demonstrate the existence of any sort of spiritual being. It stands to reason that proving that such a being is out of the question, and thus, we have to "come to believe" in a different way.

Perhaps we can follow a different tack, a different method of reasoning which does not require us to abandon the rules of logic, but which still permits us to attain something we seek. Having reached Step 1, we have recognized that on our own, we seem unable to kick this habit – whatever it may be. We have tried to quit, only to resume that habit again and again. In this sense, we know that this addiction, this habit, is already stronger than we are. But when we sit at meeting after meeting, we are faced with people who have seemingly undergone profound transformation in their own lives. This can mean that only one of two things is true: either we are sicker than they are, and we are helpless, or they were able to find something that enabled them to overcome something that was more powerful than they.

If we sit through more meetings and seek to identify with these people who speak, rather than to compare our situation to theirs, we shall see in short order that we are no sicker than many who have recovered. Thus, the only possible explanation for their recovery was something that was able to help them overcome what we, heretofore, have not been able to overcome on our own strength. It is not a faulty logic which presumes that they were able to enlist the aid of some power greater than them, and if such a power is available to others, it must be available to us as well. Thus we have a completely rational and logical way to come to believe that a power greater than us is indeed able to restore us to sanity.

## Step 2 Ritual

Where Step 2 involves the recognition that there is a power greater than ourselves, this ritual helps us to attain that knowledge in a tangible sense. Our goal is to recognize that there is something that exists beyond us, and that this being(s) is desirous of our well-being.

Find a forested place, away, as much as possible from the sounds of the city. Make sure that you can dress appropriately for the weather. Place yourself where you can see the sky, the trees and whatever wildlife might be visible. If it's the winter and there is snow, you may see the tracks of many animals.

As you are there, begin to meditate on what force it might be that keeps each of these creatures sustained. Our logical minds might say that biological processes alone compel these creatures to multiply, to seek out food, to reproduce and so forth. But when we look at pollution, hunting, the encroachment of human "civilization", animals getting hit in the roadway – why don't these creatures despair and diminish? We might gather that they have no nature to do so; we might suggest that they have no intellect with which to feel despondent. But if this is lacking, then what intellect is there to persevere? As much as we might claim that these creatures lack, they seem to have faith - the faith that all that they endure is worthwhile, the faith that there is a reason to go on.

The tree which loses its leaves in the darkness of winter has faith that come spring there will be a reason to bloom once again. The bears that hibernate in winter know that there will be a reason to awaken in the spring. The squirrel, eating its stash of nuts through the winter, does not despair because she knows there will be more and abundant food when the snow melts. Without knowing who is providing, each of these creatures knows that *something* is providing. They do not despair because they have trust.

We, too, can have faith. We, too, can have the assurance that our needs, in overcoming this addiction, will be met. We know that others have trod the road we're on, and have done what we, at least until now, may not have been able to do. But as generation after generation of wild creature is able to survive and thrive, by following the actions of previous generations, so to, will we, by following the actions of those who came before us, be able to remain in sobriety.

Sitting in the midst of nature, we remain in the midst of whatever force this might be. We don't need to know what or who this is – biological or spiritual, it is certainly a force, a power greater than us. We recognize that the only thing we're asked at this time is to believe that it exists. We don't have to define it. We don't have to prove it to others. We merely have to acknowledge that it does, indeed, exist. We realize in the midst of nature that this is not a bridge too far.

Stay for a while in the quiet, and experience all of this. Let the trust that all of nature has permeate your own being, and when it has done so, thank nature for sharing it with you. If it is your way, leave an offering and thank the Gods and Goddesses of that place for showing you how all of nature, and now you as well, can trust.

# Step 3

### *Made a decision to turn our will and our lives over to the care of the Divine and our own highest self.*

This is a step that turns many who are part of a minority religion away from the Twelve Step programs of recovery. It is the second minefield. In many programs, it is the first step that mentions God, and it speaks of God as a singular and as a male. In its original form, it reads "Made a decision to turn our will and our lives over to the care of God, as we understood him". Many who are not Christian (and many who are) miss the words "as we understood him". We fail to remember or recognize that these words were written by Christian American men in the early part of the 20th century, and that God was spoken of quite differently then. We also forget, or rather many of us have never even heard, that Bill W. and Dr. Bob really did try to create a program of recovery that was accessible to all, regardless of religious affiliation. No, we hear the words "God" and "him", and we "know" that this is a Christian program. We suspect that sooner or later, we'll get invited to a church; that sooner or later, we'll be expected, if not required, to bow down to the same god as the rest of the folks we meet in the halls of recovery.

What are the facts? Well, the fact is that the majority of Americans do identify as Christian. In any group that comprises a representative sampling of American society, you'll find that about 70% will identify as Christian. Throughout the West, this number will probably hold within a few percentage points. It will typically be lower in societies that are more modern or progressive, but it's fairly high. Programs such as Alcoholics Anonymous, Narcotics Anonymous and others do represent fairly well a sampling of the larger population.

So, to whom do these groups expect you to turn your will and your life over to? None other but the deity or higher power of your own choosing. The Twelve Step programs are not religious programs. Religion is the means whereby we express our spirituality, but our religion is not our spirituality. Our spirituality may be likened our bodies, and our religion likened to our clothing. The religion, like our clothing, is what people may see, but our spirituality gives the underlying shape and substance. Our religion, like our clothing, can be flattering or not; it can be beautiful or ugly and dirty, and a style that works wonders for one person may well not work for another. But at this stage, religion has little to do with anything. Step 3 is nothing but a decision, an agreement between you and the higher power that you believe is capable of restoring you to sanity.

## Making a decision

Step 3 is about more than merely deciding that we're going to give our will and our lives over to the care of the Gods and Goddesses, Lord and Lady, or whatever deities we choose to trust. In Step 3, we actually offer ourselves up to that care. It's much more than an intellectual assent, much more than a mere thought-experiment, and as such is an exercise in letting go of our wills. This is a great step out in trust, but if we do it well we will discover that it is not a trust that is empty. It is truly a trust that will bear fruit. The question, of course, is how exactly do we make this decision, and what shape does it take?

There have been four editions of the book *Alcoholics Anonymous*, but the first 164 pages have remained the same throughout each edition. When someone points to something in the first 164 pages, so long as it's an English copy of that text, you're sure to find it. These 164 pages are the embodiment of the Twelve Step program of recovery and are the source material for every Twelve Step program that followed. On page 63 of the book one can find a prayer in which this decision is made. It's written in much the same language as the King James Bible. Perhaps people were more familiar with that language in 1939, but to many people today, the words "thee", "thy" and "wilt" don't necessarily evoke a feeling of reverence as they once did. To many, they are simply archaic forms. Others may be moved by such language. I recall watching Princess Diana's funeral and hearing Tony Blair read from the Christian Bible. He read from Paul's first letter to the Corinthians, that section known as the "Hymn to Love". Personally I don't have a problem with 18th century English, but hearing him speak these words, they came alive. Even though the words might not have been said the way we say them every day (with "speakest" instead of "speak", with the letters "th" at the end of verbs) what really mattered was the way they were spoken, the emotion that was behind them.

I heard someone once say "Never tell a story unless you believe it completely." My grandfather used to say "Always say what you mean and always mean what you say." This is especially good advice as we approach Step 3. Just as anyone can pick up a spell book and repeat the words, repeated words are not a spell; neither are they a prayer. Anyone could pick up a copy of the Big

Book (as the text of *Alcoholics Anonymous* is known), turn to page 63, and read the prayer that appears there. Saying and doing are quite different things. I could, even as a Pagan, go to a Christian church, say the sinner's prayer and go up to the altar at an altar call. This would not make me a Christian. Words are quite capable of being empty. Any of us can say or promise anything; it's what we do afterward that counts, or what we put behind those words as we say them. A story told in truth, by one who believes it and feels it and lives it will have far more impact on the one hearing it than would the same story recounted as merely an anecdote.

When we make a decision to turn our will and our lives over to the care of our higher power, whomever that might be, if it is half-hearted, if it is done without expectation, without sincerity, without commitment, it is as if it is not done at all. This doesn't mean that we offer our will and never again become willful; it doesn't mean that our decision is perfect and perfectly kept all the time; but it does mean that we truly mean what we say and that we intend to live by this decision.

The prayer on page 63 in the Big Book of Alcoholics Anonymous reads "God, … Relieve me of the bondage of self, that I may better do Thy will. Take away my difficulties, that victory over them may bear witness to those I would help of Thy Power, Thy Love, and Thy Way of Life. May I do Thy will always!" This isn't a Pagan prayer, per se, but, with a bit of modification it could be, and it is a good prayer. It is a prayer that says that we now have a purpose that comes from somewhere beyond ourselves, a higher purpose. It is a statement of the recognition of the fact that we can be better, more than what we are, and that we are willing to give ourselves over to the power or being that is capable of helping us become better. It is filled neither with pridefulness nor with false humility. It speaks of a hope and perhaps even an expectation of victory, which in our case is freedom from the bondage of addiction. Its only problem is that it may not be "our" prayer. But again, by maintaining the sentiments and changing the words, we could if we so desired make it ours. As Pagans, it's good to remember that no religion was ever created in a vacuum — all of them are derived from previous or contemporary religions. If we find a prayer that speaks to us, there is no shame in using it or in modifying it for our own purposes.

We've all seen the plays and motion pictures where the verbally clumsy boy seeks the help of one who is able to woo through words alone. The clumsy boy asks his silken-tongued friend for the words that will win the heart of the maiden he desperately desires. He repeats poetry and prose that are given to him, but these are not his words. He may be expressing emotion, but not his thoughts. The girl is falling for the message, rather than the messenger, and often feels deceived when she discovers the truth. The boy using the words of another discovers that he, in the end, has lost yet another chance at true happiness.

Such is the case with prayer; unless the words spoken are words that have meaning to us, they aren't ours. As the story-teller said, don't tell the story (in this case the prayer) unless you truly believe it. Better than to simply recite a prayer that isn't yours, write your own. We don't need poetry that flows as if it came from the pen of Shakespeare to get our message across, and most of us aren't capable of such writing anyway. Such a prayer doesn't need rhyme or rhythm; what it needs is truth and sincerity. We are expressing what we are giving in this step. We are making a sacrifice of our wills, and offering our lives. In exchange, we will receive back our lives, only free from the bondage of addiction. If we wanted, we could simply rephrase the existing prayer and offer it to our patron deity. It might read "Blessed Brighid, I offer myself to you, to build with me, and to do with me as you wish. Remove from me this bondage of self, so that I might better do your will. Take from me my difficulties so that victory over them will show others your power, love and way of life. May I do your will always."

That was quite simple to do, and may be in a language which is more suitable to someone today. The point here is to offer up to deity a prayer that truly expresses what is in *our* hearts; to offer up our intentions rather than someone Else's words. It doesn't have to be fancy or flowery, but it must be true, and we must believe it. As in all magick, intent is the operative word; without intent whatever we say is void.

## Our Highest Self

Pagans have many different views of Deity and of self. Our dictionary is replete with terms to describe Deity and our relationship with the Divine. There is Monotheism, Polytheism, Henotheism, Animism, Deism, Pantheism, Panentheism … we can literally come up with dozens of terms such as these, but they all refer to different beliefs as to the nature of Deity. Some Pagans believe in many Gods (Polytheism) and some believe that all Gods are one, essentially resolving to a monotheism. So when we speak to another Pagan, we're unlikely to agree completely even as to the nature of such a being. But fortunately these tend to be side issues, and we allow each other the latitude to express our own beliefs and look to the principles we're trying to express rather than the constructs that form the system of belief.

Some Pagans believe in reincarnation, and others don't. Some believe that there is something of us that survives beyond this life, and others believe that once we die, all that is self is gone. So any discussion of a higher self, and the relationship of that self to any Divine being is fraught with difficulties – it is nearly impossible to speak any position and to find complete agreement in any room. What follows may resonate with you – or it may not, but I hope that the principles will at least make sense.

When we speak of our Highest Self, we do not speak of the mundane desires of the body. Many Pagans and spiritualists recognize that what exists in body and mind is merely a reflection of a multi-dimensional being, and many exercises that we involve ourselves with are designed to increase the connection between the mundane self and the true, higher self. It is on this level that we work most closely with Deity. It is the physical body and the physical mind that are subject to addictions and mental illness and disease. The higher self is unaffected by such things. And so it makes sense, when embracing recovery, to contact not only deity, but to also seek to know the will of our true and higher self. Many of us have come to Earth with a mandate, a contract or a purpose, and knowing that purpose, and working toward it is a large portion of our recovery.

Once again, we remember Aleister Crowley, the great ceremonial mage who wrote the words that ultimately became the Wiccan Rede. His words were "Do what thou wilt shall be the whole of the law. Love is the law, love under will". In Wicca, it was revised to "An it harm none, do what thou will." In either version we encounter the concept of will. In Crowley's language, will is not mere desire – our wants, our likes, our Earthly passions. The concept of will in Thelema refers much more to our true purpose – our life's calling. One might consider this will our higher self. It is this purpose which conforms to any Divine purpose. And thus, as we err in our daily lives, we stray not only from any Divine plan, but from our own purpose as well.

In recovery, we seek to know the plan or will of our Gods and Goddesses, and we seek also to know our own higher will. When we decide to turn our will and our lives over to the care of the Divine, and to our own higher will, we are recognizing that we have fallen astray of our own purpose; the path we are on is not the one we had contracted with for this particular lifetime. We are further recognizing that there is likely something far better available for us.

Perhaps we are all here to learn certain lessons – maybe we are here to undergo some experience – but any teacher with experience will know that students learn different ways depending on their particular backgrounds, constitutions or abilities. Trying to teach science or mathematics or literature to any two students can be a very different experience because those two students may learn differently. It's possible that we are experiencing addiction, mental illness or that we love a particular individual with these characteristics because there is something in this particular situation that we are destined to learn in this lifetime. Getting in touch with our higher self and with our Gods and Goddesses may be our way of stating that we are now ready, having experienced the pain of that lesson, to experience a re-birth through the process of recovery. In Step 3, we are acknowledging that there must be cooperation between our daily self, our higher self, and whichever Gods and Goddesses we work best with. We acknowledge that there is much more than just "me" in the equation, and that as far down this hole as we may have come, it's going to take more than "me" to work our way out. We have recognized that we're at the bottom, but we also know that we can call out – that someone is listening and will respond. The hole we've dug may be deep, but there is a ladder or a rope that will be provided for us at the very moment we ask. We also know that the work isn't complete, and we may have a treacherous climb ahead, but the days of going it alone are gone for as long as we're willing to trust those who have now answered the call for assistance.

# Step 3 Practical Application

In some ways we do ourselves a disservice when we grow up; and as parents, we might be perpetuating that disservice to our children. We have an attitude that "grown-ups" are those people who are able to do things on their own. It seems that asking for help is a weakness. We go from wanting to ride the bicycle ourselves to believing that there is little reason to ask for help in most anything. Of course there are exceptions – some objects are simply too large or heavy to move alone. Nobody is going to feel inferior or weak because they can't move a piano without help. But all too often asking for help seems to be a sign of weakness.

Along with this, it seems that our culture has taught us a false equivalence. For many of us, asking for help implies that we are asking someone to do something in our stead. "Can you help me change my tire" has become a passive-aggressive way of saying "Will you change my tire for me?"

In Step 3, we place our trust in a higher power, and in so doing, ask that higher power for help. We ask that this power do for us what we cannot do for ourselves, but not to do for us what we are capable of doing for ourselves. When we help another, we ought not to be doing their job, but we should be providing the assistance necessary to enable them to do their job. There is an important distinction between the two.

Providing help to another still leaves that person who has been helped room for pride and satisfaction in a job well-done. Doing their job for them leaves them empty. Our Gods and Goddesses do not seek, when we ask them for help, to do the job for us. We don't have a higher power that wants us weak, impotent and dependent; rather Deity delights in us when we succeed, having performed a task that at first blush seemed quite impossible.

Our higher power is there, as is a parent, to help; but they have no desire to do for us what we *should* do for our self. In nature, no higher power is there to place the nuts where they will be convenient for the squirrels come winter. It's not the squirrel's job to produce the winter's food, but it is their job to properly gather and store it.

The Gods and Goddesses, our higher powers, *will* help us and guide us and afford us support and balance. But they won't do the entire job. They desire that in the end, we have something to call our own, that we have something to be proud of as well. The father who never lets go of his daughter's bicycle for fear that she'll fall has given his daughter little in the end. In keeping her safe he's deprived her of the satisfaction of doing something on her own.

But a good father will also set down some rules: early on will be the admonition to wear a helmet when riding, to not venture out on our own before we're ready, to avoid busy streets and so forth. Asking for help implies that we're ready to take certain direction and to play by certain rules. These rules may be individual, because we are all different, but they won't be entirely ambiguous.

Twelve Step programs have people available who will be our sponsors. These are people who have trod the road we're on before. They know the pitfalls. They aren't there as the *Vox Dei*, or Voice of God, but they are the voice of experience, and our higher power may speak to us, on occasion, through them.

It's up to each of us to recognize when we're asking for help and when we're asking someone to do the entire job for us. In Step 3 we're that little girl asking the father to teach us to ride a bicycle. We can know that our higher power will help us to learn balance, but that at some point we'll be doing at least part of the job our self. Our job is to recognize what our part is, to know when to rely on help, and to know that it's sometimes dangerous to venture out on our own before we're ready.

Early on, like the child learning to ride a bicycle, we may need a great deal of support and our higher power, through our sponsor, friends, family and others in the program of recovery, may hold us up most if not all of the time. But a wise parent knows to let go at just the right time, and sooner or later we'll find that we are using less and less support and that we are learning to stand on our own two feet. Where we had once stood in quicksand we've been led to dry and solid Earth.

## Step 3 Ritual

This ritual is one that might work better with some help. This is fitting because in this step we have asked for help. When we ask for help, we need to rely on the person who is offering that help. If it's at all possible, try to find someone else who has been through this program and who has worked through this text to help you.

What you will need for this ritual is a stream over which is a narrow makeshift bridge, or perhaps a small pool and some cinderblocks which support a beam above the pool. The beam or bridge should be solid enough to support the weight of two people safely and wide enough to have sure footing. If none of this is available, use your imagination and come up with something similar.

In asking for help, we recognize that we need to trust. Trust is not a skill that comes easy to many of us, but it is necessary for survival, especially for the addict or alcoholic. When you have found the bridge or erected your own over a pool, you will be blindfolded and the individual helping you will lead you over this bridge. You are entirely dependent on this person so as not to fall. This is what trust is. With the blindfold, you can see neither them, nor the bridge, nor the danger beneath. Your fear is based on what you believe to exist, and on your lack of trust.

Once you have been led across, remove the blindfold, and cross again, with your own eyes. There may still be a small fear of falling, or not, but recognize now that when you were blind, you could not cross safely under your own power. You needed a power greater than yourself – in this case a power with the gift of vision – to cross that bridge. When the veil was lifted and you could again see, you were then able to cross under your own power. The gift you were given was that of one who would support you until you could support yourself.

Your friend is still there and still able to help you when you are once again in need, but now you can know with certainty that you are able to walk safely, across this obstacle at least, on your own two feet. But you have also gained the confidence that when another obstacle is in your path and you are unsure of your way, that you are not in danger so long as you rely on what help is available.

## Step 4

### *Made a searching and fearless moral inventory of ourselves.*

No enterprise can be successful without a knowledge of its assets and liabilities. Every business needs to know to whom money or product is owed, and from whom debts are to be collected. Our own lives are much like a business enterprise – we accumulate debts and we dispense to others our time, energy and effort as well. Some of us view our debts and credits as Karma, and most all agree that there is some sort of ledger sheet kept somewhere. Words like "they had it coming" suggest that there is somewhere, somehow, a settling of accounts.

Most Pagans are familiar with this sort of accounting, but many of us don't really know how to go about insuring that the things we do are working in our favor. Many of us hope that if we're nice enough, things will work out in the end. But how do we know that we're "nice enough"? And what do we do about the time before we actually sought to "be nice"? It is in Step 4 that we actually take a close and detailed look at who we are, and who we've been. What have been our motives? Have we honestly tried to do what is best for us and for those around us? Are we really as honest, as humble, as altruistic as we like to believe?

Some of us might view ourselves with negativity, disdain and even contempt, thinking that little good can come of us. We might believe that we are worthless, that we have hurt so many in our past that there is little chance, if any, of redemption. But there is a saying that we are likely to hear in the halls of recovery. It goes "You're not that good at being that bad." When we are in the midst of working Step 4, those of us who are prone to feelings of grandiosity will likely to discover that we're not that good at being that good either. If we're gaining in the ability to see things as they really are, what we'll find is that none of us are qualified for either sainthood or to be the anti-Christ. We are all people who have managed to do good and ill, but still desiring to do greater and greater good.

Just as no business can start manufacturing anything until it has the necessary components or ingredients, we're not going to be able to make a start on the changes we need to make in our lives until we know what we have to work with. The business needs an inventory of its raw ingredients, and so do we. Every business tracks its assets and obligations on some sort of balance sheet. This sheet contains debits and assets – moneys owed and spent, and accounts that have been paid or are receivable. It is from this information that a business knows if it made a profit or if it lost money. It is from this information that investors determine, in part, if a particular company is worth investing in.

And so in Step 4 we look fearlessly at our self, at our life, at what we've done, at what we've failed to do, and at our motivation for doing so. We are capable of doing this fearlessly because we are being objective, and because we are not passing judgment on our self. This is simply an exercise in accounting, but a desperately needed accounting that is long overdue.

## The Debit Side Of The Ledger

In Step 4, we once again encounter some differences between the Christian and the Pagan ways of thinking. Here we find the fundamentalist Christian and rule-based legalistic thought running headlong into the seeming relativism of the Pagan standard. In much recovery literature, one finds lists of "defects of character", compendiums of errors or of types of sin. Some of these are based on the "Seven Deadly Sins" of Lust, Gluttony, Greed, Sloth, Wrath, Envy, and Pride. These may also be known as capital sins or mortal sins. It needs to be remembered though, that these sins come from a Christian paradigm, from a rules-based morality, and may not necessarily apply to all Pagans. For example, a Pagan might look at lust and recognize that so long as it isn't out of control, lust is little more than a healthy libido. It becomes something negative when we permit our lust to rule us, or to infringe upon the rights of others. None of this is to suggest that there is no such thing as true evil, but if we look at the Seven Deadly Sins, we will recognize that each of these is nothing but a natural and healthy instinct that is merely taken to an unhealthy extreme.

If Pagans and Christians are so different, though, one may wonder how a pagan is to accomplish the moral inventory as suggested by the Twelve Steps ... does Step 4 even apply to the Pagan at all? Or can Step 4 touch something that is more universal than its Christian underpinnings? Much of Paganism does follow (in one sense or another) one rule, and much of the rest of Paganism accepts that rule as at least a good starting point for some sort of morality. This rule is the Wiccan Rede which states, "An it harm none, do what thou wilt". Some interpret this to mean "if it harms nobody, do what you want"; others shorten it to "harm none". Nearly every Pagan that I've spoken to, however, believes that each of these two interpretations misses something. Most believe the Rede to be neither as permissive or as simplistic as these two interpretations suggest. Instead, those who have taken the time and effort to ponder the Rede more deeply believe that it calls out to each of us to consider our actions carefully and thoughtfully. Put another way, the Rede might read "Consider the potential harm to every individual who may be impacted by your actions; if there is no foreseeable harm, you are free to act with liberty. If however, there is any potential harm, then you must weigh that harm against the good that will result from your actions; then act with that knowledge, and be prepared to accept the consequences (foreseen or unforeseen) from your action or inaction." This is a far taller order than simply "harm none" because it requires both foresight and the willingness to take responsibility for the outcome of our actions.

Where for Christians the completion of a moral inventory may involve the compilation of a list of offenses against God or against others – perhaps laws broken, trusts betrayed and so forth – much like the list of offenses on a traffic ticket with a tick-mark beside each violation, the Pagan must look at all his or her actions to discern the motives and consequences. A Christian might know that stealing is a sin; a Pagan might recognize that they stole in order to save the life of a person or a creature. It may have been illegal, but the wrongness of it could be another matter entirely.

When looking at the Seven Deadly Sins, the Pagan runs into another concept that seems strange or foreign to them ... that of sin itself. A "sin" is an offense against God. Many Pagans (though not all) feel that Deity, God and Goddess are entirely beyond our imagining, that nothing we could possibly do would offend them; it would be like a human being taking offense at the actions of a bacterium three inches in the ground beneath our picnic blanket. Much more important than any offense against any God are the offenses to each other, to our environment, or to the other creatures that are living on our planet. We can imagine that the Gods look at us, for the most part, as beings in a stage of growth or development – much like older generations viewing with bemusement the actions and passions of our children and grandchildren. The Pagan performing Step 4 will likely have an entirely different sort of inventory than will a Christian.

Nonetheless, we can create a real and effective inventory using the principles that are set down in Step 4. Rather than a list of possible offenses, however, a Pagan's inventory might look something like this:

➢ Have I used others for my own gain, especially without thought of what harm it might cause them?

➢ Have I put aside my own principles for immediate gratification or for temporary gain?

➢ Have I been unnecessarily wasteful of the Earth's resources?

➢ Have I set aside my integrity for financial gain, or have I placed too little value on my own time and effort?

➢ Have I sought sexual gratification without thought of safety or of the feelings or expectations of the other(s) involved?

➢ Have I endangered any others through my actions or inaction?

➢ Have I dishonored my family name or my ancestors through carelessness, action or inaction?

These are very different questions than what the Christian might come up with; they reflect an entirely different paradigm. They are fashioned from the viewpoint of a people who place greater value on intent and purpose rather than being derived from a rules-based morality. This shouldn't be taken to imply that a Pagan paradigm is better than the Christian world-view; it's simply a different way of looking at the world. It's certainly a more appropriate viewpoint for the Pagan, but then again, a rules-based approach is much better for most Christians.

## The Credit Side Of The Ledger

No inventory consisting of debits alone can assess the true value of a business; as well as what one owes, one needs to know what one has. The Christian heritage tends to emphasize humility as a virtue, and it rightly is. The trouble is that we've lost the true meaning of humility. We generally view the person who is shy, self-effacing, modest, or not acknowledging his or her achievements as the model of humility. RuneWolf spoke of humility in an article called "The Eight Virtues of the Craft", which appeared on WitchVox some years ago. He spoke of humility as taking stock of one's strengths and weaknesses, and working to "cultivate the former and to transform the latter". To truly know ourselves, we need to know those strengths as well as we know our weaknesses. From our strengths come our ability to work, to effect change in our world, to honor our ancestors, to make a difference.

The Christian view of virtue is that all that is good and righteous and of real and lasting value comes from God – man is incapable of such things on his power alone. What we do well, we do not claim as our achievement; it comes from God. We see great athletes who break world-record after world-record who then claim that it wasn't them, but the Lord. The Pagan, on the other hand, experiences a Deity who delights in our accomplishments, and who doesn't do for us what we are able to do on our own. I think that RuneWolf put it best when he said that false humility, to say "I'm really not that good" after receiving a compliment, is much like a slap in the face of Deity who gave us the talents or strength to perform such deeds. True humility, he said, is shown by acknowledging such a compliment, looking the person who offered it in the face, and simply saying "thank you".

False humility is in reality no humility at all. Most people who practice false humility are really begging for further compliments; it's gratifying to some, after saying "well, I'm not really that good" to have people disagree or protest, to hear them say "you should give yourself more credit." Many do give themselves more credit, but they downplay it to receive even more praise. Real humility suggests that we need to know where our talents lie and what our strengths really are. It is our strengths, that with the assistance of the Gods, will enable us to transform our weaknesses and bring our instincts in conformity with their true purpose. What can constitute our strengths? A short list would include such things as:

➢ Talents: music, poetry, writing, riding, gardening, etc.
➢ Abilities: Perception, empathy, vision, etc.
➢ Strengths: Physical or emotional
➢ Character: Honesty, trustworthiness, integrity, etc.

It is not prideful to take an honest look at who we are, taking note of our gifts, yet many of us feel guilty when we look at our positive qualities. To be completely humble requires that we get over this; there is no true humility in being unable to recognize our own positive traits. A lack of ability to recognize our positive characteristics is a much a lapse of integrity as any other Once we've completed this inventory though, what do we do with it? Having looked at our positive qualities, most of us will discover that our balance sheet is far from entirely written with red ink.

## Step 4 Practical Applications

Knowing who and what we are, and what we stand for, offers us advantages in every aspect of our lives. Being able to point to what we've done in our past, good or bad and accepting the consequences of those actions, gives us the ability to stand with integrity and a healthy pride, which is another word for humility. For many of us, the guilt resulting from our past actions is something we wish not to revisit, hence we hesitate on Step 4. But the benefit of the honesty afforded by the practice of taking a personal inventory is something of real value.

When we define integrity, some of us speak of a person who is impeccable - what they do is always just, always for the common or greater good. But there is another (and at this point more important) definition of integrity. Integrity is complete honesty about who we are and what we've done – good or bad, right or wrong. The first step in gaining integrity is an acknowledgment of who we are, and what we've done, right here, right now. It matters little in the way of integrity, even if we move forward doing what is right, if the actions of our past hang over us like the Sword of Damocles and we refuse to acknowledge or deal with them. For as long as we refuse to come to terms with our past, it will ever be a source of fear that taints and haunts whatever gains we may make in the present. The stress imposed from that fear of a past left uncorrected will impact our own self-worth and will sit in the pit of our stomachs as a perpetually undigested meal, sickening and weakening us. We will try, at times, to stand firm and proud, but our knees will remain weak, and we will see our pride is nothing but a mask, covering another mask, and another still, like the layers of an onion, which, when peeled away reveal that what lies beneath is shame.

Our past is something that will perpetually follow us, but it is something we can deal with and we needn't be ruled by it. One saying in Alcoholics Anonymous goes "We will not regret the past, nor wish to shut the door on it." If we choose to work at it, we can mitigate the influence our past has over us today, but in order to do that, we need to acknowledge what wreckage we've left in our wake. We are like a driver who is ticketed by the police for speeding – we can't travel back in time and retroactively alter our speed. Likewise, with our own past, we can't go back and alter the things we have done – we can't unhurt those we've hurt, but we can acknowledge that past and make whatever corrections are necessary to avoid the same error in the future.

At this point in our journey through the Twelve Steps, we may not be ready to atone for our past failings, but that isn't the task we're confronted with right now. Rather, our job, at this moment in time is to take stock of who we are and what we've done. In the recent past, we've learned that we have been helpless, that there is someone in whom we can place our trust, and we've come to believe that they can, and will help us as we confront whatever difficulties may lie ahead. Step 4 is the first seemingly dangerous ground that we will need to tread. We are going to use what we've learned in the first three steps to trust that despite our trepidation and the shakiness of our knees, we will have the strong and bracing hands of one who will walk beside us to hold us up for as long as we in need, and that we are able to trust and willing to receive that assistance.

What we can know about revisiting our past is that we are experiencing nothing new. Some of what we revisit may be unpleasant, but we have already survived it. Visiting it from the present will not destroy us. Whatever power our past has over us is merely that with which we endow it. Looking closely at our past enables us to understand each of the choices we've made, and understanding each of these choices affords us the opportunity to learn something important about who we are right now. It is necessary, as we work through Step 4, to avoid passing judgment on our selves. If we approach this step with an attitude that permits self-condemnation, we will likely fail. Instead we might endeavor to adopt the attitude of an independent auditor – one who merely takes note of facts, one who does not judge. The independent auditor has no interest in the implications of the data that she or he is collecting – the auditor's interest is in the collection and presentation of truth. If we can do this, if we can, without fear, merely look back and take notes, filling in both sides of our ledger as we do, we will be doing the job that we are tasked to do. We will have an inventory that is valuable to us as we progress through the remainder of these steps.

The practical application of Step 4 is achieved when we are able to be completely honest to our selves. As the Oracle at Delphi admonishes us to "Know Thyself", we will understand upon completion of Step 4 who we are and what we are about. This, though well into the steps already, is a starting point and a point of change in our lives. We are now in possession of the gift of insight into our own minds; we now have the tools of self-examination, and as we progress from here, we need never again be a mystery to ourselves.

# Step 4 Ritual

Any ritual for Step 4 needs to emphasize the fact that the first person we need to be honest with is our self, and that fearlessness, or at least courage, must win out over shame. This ritual will take us to a place we may not have been before, and is best done in private. Though this ritual is designed to be conducted when you first begin work on Step 4, it may be performed at any point thereafter. It is not designed to be used before you are ready to begin that work.

> For this ritual you will need:
> A full-length mirror. (Smaller ones might do, but they should be large enough to see a large portion of our body. If you don't have one handy, many stores, even second-hand shops are good places to get such a mirror.)
> A lamp or candles.
> A robe.
> A notebook.
> A pen or pencil.
> Your favorite bath/shower products.

Many of us suffer from some form of shame of self. We may have a poor body image, we might have scars, too much or too little hair. Beyond the shame we suffer from the things we've done, beyond our poor body image, we may suffer from the shame of simply being. This ritual will give us a starting point; here we will begin our personal inventory by looking at the outside first.

With this ritual, you will want to insure that you are in a place where we will not be disturbed, and where there is room to set up our mirror (or where you have one available). You may set up some quiet music if that makes you comfortable.

Begin by lighting candles (taking care that they are placed safely) or some other source of soft lighting. Standing in front of the mirror, look at yourself. Ask yourself the following questions:

> Why am I dressed the way I am?
> What does the way I dress say about me?
> Am I trying to send a message to the people around me?
> Is what I am wearing congruent with who I am?
> Do I look like the person I truly wish to be?

Write these things, and any other thoughts that come to mind in your notebook. Now begin to take off your clothing, watching yourself in the mirror as you do. Recognize that each article of clothing is not only covering you, but hiding you. Ask yourself what each article represents as you remove it, and record this in your notebook.

Now, you are standing naked in front of your mirror, exposed to yourself. Examine your body closely. Take your time, from head to toe, to record each detail and how you feel about it, but be sure to record not only the negatives, but the positives as well. In fact, if you don't have just as many positives as you do negatives, something is missing in your inventory. This is especially important for those of us who might have some sort of eating disorder; to find any real and lasting healing it is imperative that we discover and recognize those things about us that are good.

What color is your hair? Is it straight or curly? Is it artificially colored? Is it a part of your disguise? Do you wish to change it? Why, or why not?

What is your face like? Does it show the work you've done, the joys you've had or the sorrows you've experienced? Does it reflect back to you wisdom or weariness? Does it show your age well, or does it show that you've perhaps lived your life, and perhaps more than your expected share? If you could change something about your body, what might it be? Or are you happy and satisfied with who you are today?

Inside your head is your brain – the physical seat of your consciousness. How well has it served you? Obviously, you are able to read and understand this book, or you wouldn't be doing so! Do you have emotional difficulties that you deal with? Write these in your notebook. This might include whatever addiction or compulsion you are working to overcome. Obviously you have an intellect as well; how does this serve you? Do you use your mind in your job? Certainly your mind will be a part of your recovery. Write all that you discover here down in your notebook as well.

From head to toe, scan your body once more – looking for anything that you might have missed. Remember that the point isn't self-flagellation or criticism – but honesty.

When you are done, imagine yourself as you would like to see yourself, perhaps one year, or five years from now. See that person in the mirror and take note of all the details you can, and record these in your notebook, being sure to date it. When one year, or five – which ever you chose, comes about, look back to this notebook and see if the reality matches.

Keeping the image of who you wish to be in mind, and if you are able, it's time to perform a little magic. Take a shower or bath with your favorite products. As you bathe, visualize everything that is separating the you as you are, from the individual you wish to be, being washed away as if it were some still-wet, water-based paint. All the work that you have done in this process to date, and all the work that remains is leading you to the person you strive to become. The work that you begin in this step is a major part of that transformation, and today, you have begun it in earnest.

## Step 5

*Admitted to Deity, to ourselves, and to another human being the exact nature of our wrongs.*

In most Twelve Step programs, the Pagan once again encounters the word "God", and with it, in many groups, a Christian attitude. In the original form, and in most forms of the Twelve Steps, this step is worded "Admitted to God …" and it is likely that we as Pagans are finding ourselves at odds with some other Christian ideas as well. But before we despair, take a look at what we're doing and what this step in actuality implies. In Step 4, we made an inventory; in Step 5, we are called to make it, in some limited sense, a bit public. Where in Step 4 we might have thought we dismantled our ego, in Step 5 it seems that we seemingly lay waste to that ego, tossing it in the path of the wrecking-ball; we're directed to take all our dirty laundry and share it not only with deity, but with another human being. We are told that humility requires that we bare our naked soul to another human being.

When I reached this point in the steps, I'm not sure if it bothered me more because I grew up Christian, or because I was now a Pagan. As a Christian, as a Catholic, I was used to the idea of confession, even though I didn't avail myself of that particular sacrament with any frequency. I could go to the priest in a darkened confessional, separated by a screen of sorts, and have the illusion that the priest didn't know me. I would take my shopping-list of sins that were committed since the last time I had kneeled in that chamber, recite them, and receive a recipe of penance which would then absolve me of those sins. Should I die after completing that task, I would pass the test at the gate and be welcomed into paradise. I had some trust of those priests because I knew they were sworn to secrecy, and that at least some priests had gone to jail when they would not repeat what had been shared with them in those confessionals.

However, not being a Christian when I reached Step 5, this admission to another person served a different purpose; in this case, I was not seeking absolution but accountability, and a real reason to change my ways and to do better. When I did Step 5, I chose to share this list with the sponsor who was taking me through these steps. When I had accomplished this, I discovered a third reason to be accountable to another human being; I discovered that what I thought was so horrible about myself was not really that horrible, extreme or distasteful at all. Certainly I had my share of peccadilloes, but I wasn't the horrible and disgusting person I had imagined.

## Admitting Our Defects Of Character To God

Many of us believe that the Gods know our hearts; while the idea of a formal admission of our faults to deity doesn't sound bad, some of us think it's fairly unnecessary. Why should a Goddess or God, who are presumably omniscient, need to hear us relate some shopping list of faults to them? "Admitting to God" sounds almost redundant or tautological; we can't lie to Deity; and we would certainly be stupid if we expected that we had a possibility of making any divine being believe anything that is untrue! How could we possibly admit to them anything they are unaware of? The truth is that deity doesn't need us to admit anything; there is nothing that we could say that they "need" to hear. We can't tell them anything about ourselves that will surprise them. Our admission of our faults to deity is not for the sake of deity, but for our own benefit. It's important for us to hear our selves speak out loud our admission of whatever faults we might have, whatever part of our lives are in need of transformation, to our higher power. This admission is a preparatory step to the step that follows – it will prepare us to speak that truth to another human being. It plants the seed for a very transformative process. It cultivates and fertilizes within us that portion of our spirits that is becoming ready to be more fruitful than we could have before imagined.

Each of the steps is foundational to the next, and admitting to God (or rather God and Goddess) prepares us for the transformations that will occur in Steps 6 and 7.

## Admitting To Our Self

Surely this seems a simple thing; we've already made the list, we know what we've done, isn't this already an admission? In some respects it is, but I believe that this step speaks more of ownership than simple admission. It implies taking responsibility for who we are, while at the same time, not placing upon ourselves an undue and paralyzing shame for the things we've done. Most anyone who has been addicted to any substance has done things that they could likely be very ashamed of. If we wanted to, we could bury our selves and wallow in that shame and decide not to go on. We could, if we wished, feel worthless and disgusted with ourselves or, instead we can discover within ourselves a sense of dignity, self-respect and courage.

Dignity could be defined as proper application of pride. It permits us to acknowledge who we are, and enables us to be ready to accept the consequences for what we've done. It allows us to apologize when appropriate, and it doesn't back down from what is right and necessary. Dignity is what is necessary to truly admit to our selves exactly who and what we are. It's strange that, as was mentioned before, often the most difficult things to admit to self are the positive qualities.

### Admitting To Another Human Being

This is an interesting part of Step 5 because it calls to mind our Protestant tendencies. While Catholics practice a sacrament of confession or repentance in which one admits to a priest their faults, the Protestant tendency is to go directly to God, and not to another human being. Many Protestants don't believe that confession to a priest is necessary; nor do they believe that a priest can offer any sort of absolution of sins. It makes a certain sense ... if God is omniscient, doesn't he know anyway? And if absolution ultimately comes from God, why should we go to a priest; why should we need some intermediary?

As Pagans, we don't necessarily have the same concerns – we don't stand in fear of some eternal punishment, and we have no sacrament that allows us escape from the consequences of our actions. So the reasoning of Protestants for avoiding the admission of our failings to another human being does not apply to us.

Fortunately, we who are doing Step 5 are not seeking absolution; rather, what we are seeking is accountability and the opportunity to be honest with another human being – a quality many of us may have been hitherto lacking. Many of us have spent so much time and energy lying (we promised that we would quit – that this was the last time we would get high or drunk or whatever), that we possibly have difficulty with the truth when it is necessary; especially when we have to be honest with regard to a fault we have. It is far easier to ignore a situation or to lie, than to admit that we've wronged another or failed to remain sober yet again.

Being brutally honest about ourselves by relating our shortcomings to another human being is a monumental task, but it is one that pays off handsomely. If we can take this one step, and be completely candid and honest in this one situation, what possible excuse could there be for dishonesty in the future? If we can lay bare our soiled spirit to a person whom we trust and respect, why will there ever be a need to hide dirty secrets again? Honesty is a fundamental component of magick. We need to be able to trust and believe our own words; words that cannot be trusted cannot be vessels of power; they are fundamentally flawed – as ineffective as a fork when trying to eat soup. If we have cultivated within ourselves the ability to be completely honest, then our words are powerful. When we cast a spell and we know, viscerally, that our words speak only truth, that what we speak comes to definite fruition, how much more powerful is our magick then?

Being this honest with another human being is a quantum leap in our honesty; in our ability to have our words mean what we say. Honest words, spoken with power, simply cannot return void. This is a fundamental principle of magick, and it's a fundamental principle that will make the Twelve Steps work for us.

## With Whom Shall We Share?

Sharing our fifth Step may be one of the most important decisions we make in our sobriety. It's important to come face-to-face with another human being, but the decision of whom that will be must be made with great wisdom. There are qualities this person must have which will make the task easier.

The person we share all these intimate details of our lives with must be discreet; we need to trust that what we share will go no further. For that reason, many who do their fifth Steps often will choose a Catholic priest who has taken a vow not to disclose what is shared in a confessional setting. Obviously, for many Pagans, this isn't an option. But fortunately, there are many Pagan clergy available, and one might find a willing ear there. While most Pagan clergy do not take the same vows as a Catholic priest, most will understand the delicate nature of what is being asked of them and will respect our wishes. Knowing the clergy person to whom we shall share can be a benefit.

The person with whom we share should also be a person of wisdom and integrity as well, for in our reading we might find that some feedback will enable us to change long-time habits. Often we find that many of the things we thought were terrible - some of the things that made us most uncomfortable – are in no way unique and peculiar to us. It's been said that "If there is a name for it, someone else has done it. If there is a law against it, lots of people have done it." None of us are unique, and that sort of feedback can be very beneficial.

The person with whom we share should be a humble person. There is nothing worse than sharing our most intimate of issues than doing so with someone who will use this as an opportunity to engage in one-upmanship. It's good to hear that we aren't alone, but having it become a competition defeats the purpose of the exercise.

For many, the person we share with will be our sponsors. If we've chosen wisely in obtaining a sponsor, we have already developed a relationship with her or him. They have likely seen us at our worst, or we've already shared with them a good portion of our past misery. Their job is to help us grow, and sharing our 5th Step will be simply another tool to help us on that pathway. Some sponsors may not be comfortable in that role, but they might be able to direct us to another person who is.

Many of us have committed crimes. We might be discouraged from sharing with another if, for example, they are a law enforcement officer or a mandated reporter. That's understandable. But it's also important to remember that part of recovery is taking responsibility for all our actions. We may wish to put off that responsibility for a while, but any good sponsor, especially a good Pagan sponsor, will remind you that in the end, all debts must be paid.

In any case, there *is* someone with whom we can share. If you are reading this text, someone near you is willing and able to help you with Step 5.

## Step 5 Practical Application

Many of us who have experienced addiction have developed a habit in which we try to maintain some outer sense of control – we have lost integrity because what we do and what we say are very different things indeed. To be truly integrated beings, our actions must be in harmony with our words. Speaking about our actions and motivation to another human being is a tool that begins to lead us in that direction. There is likely no greater tool to achieve personal integrity than to be accountable to another human being. No other form of motivation is more powerful over our intentions than to know that we will not only be confronted with the things we have done, but we will speak them, to somebody else, with our own mouths.

In this sense, Step 5 is one of the most profound tools for personal transformation in existence. It brings us to an understanding of integrity which may have been missing in most of our lives.

Many of us recoil at the thought of expressing our peccadilloes, let alone far greater failings, to another person. It makes us uncomfortable – we feel ashamed, embarrassed, a failure. But to use a metaphor, let's pretend that we have a classic car, maybe a '65 Mustang. It's worth a great deal of money, but unfortunately, whoever painted it last did a poor job. We might keep it shiny, but unless something is done about that poor paint job, the car will rust. And our classic car may deteriorate right before our eyes. The first step of restoring that car is to strip all that old paint off so that a new and proper coat of primer and paint can be applied.

In achieving personal integrity, that first step is stripping ourselves bare so that we can see what is truly beneath the facade. Getting honest, first with Deity, and then with another human being is that "stripping of the paint". We feel exposed because we are exposed. But once so laid bare, we're able to clothe ourselves with truth rather than a false image. We need no longer pretend, but we can live with integrity and truth as the motivating factors of our lives.

One of the realities about the Twelve Step programs is that few people ever fully commit to paper their fourth step. Some may go part way, but many will skip a great number of the more embarrassing details, precisely because they know that in Step 5, if they wish to assiduous about this program, they will have to be honest with another human being. The irony is that omission during Steps 4 and 5 doesn't constitute a lie or a failure to anyone but ourselves. These steps are the first moments in our lives in our endeavor to make honesty and accountability guiding principles rather than merely lofty but unattainable goals in our lives.

We may gloss over parts of our lives when doing Step 4. We may skip over some embarrassing lines when reading Step 5 to another human being. But doing so means that we are still hiding, we are still being dishonest, and we still lack integrity. And it is indeed perilous try to convince ourselves that we have actually completed these steps while knowing that we have lied, once again, to ourselves. If this is the sort of behavior we are engaging in while doing the steps, we are engaging in the same behavior that compelled us to tell our loved ones that "we won't drink again" (or drug again or whatever habit we might have had). When we gloss over our past, we skimp on our path to sobriety, at our own peril.

## Step 5 Ritual

Because there are a number of different approaches to Step 4, when we reach Step 5, the amount of content people have can vary quite a lot. Some of us come into Step 5 with a few sheets of paper, while others have full notebooks or even binders. A shorter list doesn't mean that one skimped – it may simply be a different method of accounting. Where some people simply write down what their failings are, others take note of each instance of each failing that they can remember, writing down the who, what, when, where and why of each and every instance. In any case, this ritual may take longer to accomplish depending on how much you have to read. If it will take you hours or days, you may wish to spread this out over a period of time.

First, obtain an image of the deity with whom you wish to share your inventory. This may be a statue, a painting or some other image. You may be indoors or out, depending on how you typically approach your deity, but it should be in a private setting, outside the ear-shot of others, and away from the noises of the city.

Meditating on the image of your deity, visualize yourself in their actual presence – see not the image, but the Goddess or the God you are working with. Explain your purpose: that you are here to expose your true self with the hope of living with real integrity. As you begin to read, do so with your ears open to what your Goddess or God has to say in return. In doing this reading, do so aloud, as it will be done with another human being. We are preparing our self, forming the words, making the sounds – much as an actress does when rehearsing her lines.

When you speak to Deity, you may wish to have another notebook with you to write down their comments to you. They may have suggestions as to how you might avoid the situations or circumstances that led you to such errors in the future. They may have advice as to how you might reconcile with people you may have harmed. Communication with Deity should always be a dialogue. If we speak, but don't listen, we are missing out on the most important part of the exchange.

Having had a dialogue with our Goddess or our God, we have now prepared our self to engage with another human being. We have already spoken the words, and the second time we do something, it is often easier than the first. When performing this ritual, you may bring some object with you – perhaps a stone or a crystal – or you may find one where you are actually performing this ritual. If you need some object to touch, which will give you courage when finding the person with whom to share, or in the actual sharing of your writing, ask your Deity to bless this object for you, and keep it with you for the task ahead.

When you have concluded, thank your Goddess or God for being there and hearing your words.

## Step 6

### *Were entirely ready to effect, with the help of Deity, a profound change in our character.*

When we approach Step 6, we have, by this time, been granted a gift of humility. We have examined our self, we have come to terms with the fact that we have weaknesses, and while doing so, have discovered that we aren't devoid of a significant reserve of strength as well. We have learned that real and true humility requires that we acknowledge strength as well as weakness. We are becoming more integrated, more possessing of integrity. But now, being faced with our deficiencies, we become ready to transform our selves to make of our lives what they can be – to weave in the missing colors in the tapestry that is our lives, to clean away and to correct what is deficient or worn. In Step 6, we recognize that while we may not be able to change our character with the power of will alone, we are willing to effect, with the help of the Goddesses and the Gods, such changes that could bring our actions to accord with our highest will. We become prepared to pray, or possibly to work some magick.

My prayers, at one point in my life, were for a desire for change. I knew that there were things in my life that needed to change, and I wanted to *want* to change, but didn't know how to summon the actual desire for change. This is our goal in Step 6; we are seeking in earnest that desire that will bring about transformation. Though this seems like a simple process, something that we can achieve by simple intellectual assent or by voicing our desire, it is a great deal more than this. Once again, it can't be a casual admission, but to have any significant effect, it needs to be expressed with honesty, sincerity and feeling.

I have stated that the Twelve Steps are a form of magick because I believe that's precisely what they are. Each step either prepares us, raises energy, or directs energy, and finally as we shall see if we complete them, in the last step we will ground our selves through our work with others. Step 6 is one in which energy is raised for use in the following step. The amount of energy that we permit ourselves to raise through the act of becoming entirely ready to experience a transformative change will have a direct impact on our ability to experience that change. The tool of choice in Step 6 is meditation; we need to find within ourselves the desire to change. We might at this point gather up the inventory that we completed in Step 4 and look for those things that will indicate to us our need for transformation. As Pagans, we should also look at our strengths and become entirely ready to have these bolstered as well, and to become ready to commit to their use once we begin our process of transformation.

Each of us who has joined a Twelve Step program has done so because some part of our life has been unmanageable or unworkable. One of the most common comments heard in the rooms of recovery is "it just wasn't working anymore". We recognized and admitted this in the very first step. As we have progressed, we have learned that one single area of unmanageability – our addiction, compulsion or habit – was not a solitary issue. It affected all (or at very least many) areas of our lives ... and so we discovered in Step 4 that we had many other aspects of our lives that required change in order to make our lives more fulfilling.

Willingness is not always the easiest state of being to achieve. Many of us who were addicted to a substance or activity, long before we actually did something about it, can recall a time in our lives in which we knew that what we were doing was harming us – we knew it was wrong and contrary to the highest good for our lives, but we couldn't find or muster within us the desire to quit. It was as if we "wanted to want" to quit but had no idea how to simply want it. This is what Step 6 is about – it's about discovering willingness.

Nothing ever begins in our own lives, by our own hands, until we have achieved a state of willingness. Unless we are unconscious and some medical procedure is performed to save our life, physicians require our permission to perform a procedure. If we are sued for failure to pay a creditor, the judge will most often see a contract we signed, indicating our assent to either pay, or to be subjected to legal proceedings; we might feel as if we are being coerced, but we were initially willing and we were the initiators on at least some level. When we get a license to drive a vehicle, we are agreeing to follow the rules of the road; we are also willing to assume the very real risks in doing so. In each of these cases, and many more in our lives, we have stated that we are ready, willing, to follow the rules, and to accept whatever consequences may follow should we fail to adhere to those rules or if we are injured through some accident or through neglect by another. Whether we admit it or not, we consented – we were willing.

Likewise, when we achieve something of note we demonstrate willingness. The runner who completes a marathon had previously become willing to endure a great amount of physical distress – physical pain is part and parcel of the necessarily rigorous training for such events as is evidenced by the number of runners who must ice their knees to reduce swelling, who collapse out of exhaustion and so on. But they demonstrate this willingness because the prize attained at the end, even if it is merely completing such an arduous event, is deemed worthwhile. Those who design and build our great buildings and bridges and other structures, while not enduring physical discomfort as a runner or some other athlete, still demonstrate willingness in that they have taken on whatever the task may be. We *all* need to make a decision and to come to a state of willingness before we are able to achieve anything. There are few occasions in human existence where willingness is unnecessary or which plays no part, and most such moments are quite likely to be very unpleasant. The person in a persistent vegetative state, a prisoner of war ... individuals such as these are likely to experience fewer opportunities to demonstrate willingness than most of us, as their ability to act autonomously is severely restricted. But each and every act that we initiate is preceded by some state of willingness, some choice that we have made to perform an act or to accept the resulting consequences from a failure to have taken some action.

The task at hand with Step 6 is the readiness to experience transformation. We are presented with the opportunity, having discovered our weaknesses in Step 4 and having admitted them to Deity and another human being in Step 5, to begin to work toward a new life which is unfettered and unhindered by those weaknesses. Through the transformative Magick of these Twelve Steps and with the help of Deity, we are presented with the means and the opportunity to adopt a way of life which removes the yoke of inability. But means and opportunity are not sufficient. These stand before us, as a gift in the hands of a friend; they are offered only, but not forced upon us. If we wish to avail ourselves of this opportunity, we must extend our hands as well and take ownership of that which is offered. That is the essence of willingness as it applies in Step 6.

## Step 6 Practical Application

The practical result of Step 6 is the knowledge that willingness is an essential component in each and every action that we take – even if that action seems, at first blush, accidental. It implies responsibility as well as desire in just about everything we are likely to experience.

Using the experience of driving an automobile again, if we get behind the wheel of a car, we have become willing to accept the responsibility and the consequences of doing so. There can be no personally mitigating factors. (While insurance companies and courts may find us not at fault in certain circumstances, whatever does happen to us, we have ultimate spiritual responsibility simply because we have placed ourselves in whatever situations we discover ourselves in.) If we discover that it's icy ... we were willing; we got behind the wheel. If we were tired, or under the influence ... we were willing under those circumstances. We find that sometimes, we try to weasel out of our responsibility – we might suggest that we were unaware of conditions, but we all know that weather or driving conditions can change. We can't blame a change in weather conditions for our desire to experience something. The failure to take into account the possibility of changing conditions is itself a choice, and it is a choice that many of us make relatively often.

And just as willingness is implied when we experience negative consequences, so is it necessary if we are to experience anything that is good in our lives. We require willingness to experience growth and positive change. The difference, as it applies to personal transformation rather than an activity such as driving an automobile, is that we are using it to effect a change in our being. We are looking for something much more significant than going to the store for a carton of milk. Here in Step 6 we are becoming willing with full knowledge that our lives are about to change, and this can be a terrifying proposition. But it is much more than a simple adventure – it is a rite of passage. For many, it is the first time in our lives that we look to the future and say, rather than "What do I want to do?" ... "Who do I desire to be?"

We have before us our inventory with both sides of the ledger in plain view; in black ink and red. Now it's time to begin the vitally important task of balancing the books. It is our choice, right now, to begin the work, or to close the book and wait for some future date. But as any business owner knows, closing the book does not mean that creditors will cease calling. All debts become due and payable, and in our lives, our weaknesses do not transform of their own accord. We do not change who we are until we are willing to do so.

## Step 6 Ritual

Our ritual in step 6 will be an exercise in mindfulness. We will pick one day in the near future in which we examine how our wills determine each and every action we take. In so doing, we will learn that we have a great deal more influence and authority over our own lives than we might have suspected prior to this exercise.

### Preparation

Choose the day on which you will perform this ritual. Try to choose for yourself a day in which nothing else is planned. To make this easier, have your meals prepared (or at least have the ingredients at hand with which to prepare your meals). Try to choose a place where you can be alone and undisturbed for the entire day. The reason why you might wish to have meals planned, and why you wish not to be disturbed will be more apparent as you discover the goal of the day.

If you have never practiced mindfulness meditation, or at least not on a regular basis, you might wish to avoid driving during your first attempts. It is difficult, at first, to practice this sort of mindfulness while operating a vehicle or operating dangerous machinery. But as you practice mindfulness and make it a part of your spiritual practice, you may find that it will actually improve your ability to perform and appreciate everyday tasks.

### A Day Of Mindfulness

The goal of this one-day ritual is to be mindful that willingness is required for each and every action no matter how mundane or banal, that you perform. As you spend this day you will be in constant meditation. For some, this may be a form of meditation that you are not familiar with, but it is meditation. You will likely begin your day by waking in your bed. Be mindful that even the simple action of rolling on to your side to silence the alarm requires a degree of willingness to reach over to the clock and to press the button – you could just lay there until it silenced itself, but you choose not to, and you will yourself to act. Choosing which button to press was an exercise in will – you could have pressed the snooze button instead of the one which completely silences the alarm.

As you go about your day, take the time to be contemplative, and notice that before each and every conscious act that you perform, you are making a choice – you are becoming *willing* to do each act. When it's time for breakfast, notice that you feel hunger, and that you have become *willing* to satisfy that hunger. You choose to eat something, so you become *willing* to go to your kitchen – you become *willing* to open the pantry door, and do so; you become *willing* to look to the cereal, and do so; you become *willing* to take the cereal from the pantry, and do so; to pour some into the bowl, and do so. Likewise, retrieving the milk from the refrigerator, a bowl from the cupboard, a spoon from the drawer – each and every action requires *willingness*. And then it is time to eat the cereal. You become *willing* to put the spoon into the bowl, and do so. You become *willing* to lift some of the cereal to your mouth, and do so. You become *willing* to open your mouth, to insert the spoon, to close your lips, and to remove the spoon, and do each of these in turn. Then you become *willing* to chew, and to swallow. When you have finished breakfast, you *become willing* to place the used bowl in the sink or dishwasher, and you will either to wash it then, or take care of it later. Take the time at each and every juncture to notice well your own willingness. *Examine that willingness – what does it feel like? What does it look like. You may discover that willingness is becoming real and tangible to you.*

At some point in the morning you may choose to shower. Again, take note of each action, and the *willingness* which precedes it. You become *willing* to turn the faucets on, to check the temperature of the water, to undress and enter the shower, to towel off and dry yourself, to find clean clothes to wear. At each and every juncture willingness and a decision to act, is involved.

You may choose to watch a movie, or listen to some music during the day, and each and every separate action that leads up to doing so is a separate, individual choice. You *will* to look at your collection of movies or music, and do so. You *will* to permit your eyes to focus on a single selection, and do so. You *will* to retrieve a selection and to look at its content, and do so. You may like that selection, and *will* to watch or listen, or you may not, and will to return it to your library, and do accordingly. Then you *will* to put the selection in your player and do so.

You may choose to take a walk somewhere, and in doing so you notice that again that each and every step involved in taking a walk is an act of will. You *will* to put on a jacket if it's cold, and do so (as well as clothes and sneakers if you haven't done so yet). You *will* to go to the door and do so – to open the door and do so. And each and every step that you take along your walk is an act of will – a decision made, and only after that will is the next step taken in the direction chosen.

As you go about your day and continue to practice and notice your willingness, you just might notice that prior to having become willing, you have chosen to be willing. You have now discovered the hidden secret that is the key and the solution to the vexing difficulty of "wanting to want" – that feeling that was so key to urging each of us toward what we were all looking for when we first realized that our lives had become unmanageable. You have finally found that the pathway to willingness is not through fate or chance, it's not something that is attainable to those fortunate few, but it is something that is ultimately under your own control. You have held the keys all along, and you no longer need to search for them.

At the end of the day, you can conclude the ritual of mindfulness by closing your eyes and willing a peaceful slumber.

# Step 7

### *Humbly implored Deity to help us effect that change.*

It's curious that step seven is the shortest in number of words of all the twelve steps, yet it has the most remarkable impact of all the steps thus far in our recovery. The preceding steps have prepared us for what will ultimately result in a dramatic transformation in our beings. We have, to this point, discovered that our lives are unmanageable, that there is a way out, and a path to a healthy life; we've taken stock of exactly who we are, and who we might become. We've come to accept that we could change and have become willing to have our weaknesses transformed. Here in Step 7 we finally look to Deity in humility, strength and confidence and say "Please furnish me with the strength to change my inner nature in accordance with my highest will." There is a passage in the Christian Bible where a man was imploring Jesus to heal his son. Jesus said that if the man would but believe, his son would be healed. The man was concerned because Jesus' disciples were unable to help, but still he suspected Jesus might be able to, and the man replied "Lord, I believe. Help my unbelief."

At this stage of our recovery, we might be something like that man. We have become willing to change, we have become willing to seek the assistance of Deity, and intellectually we comprehend that the strength and wherewithal to change does exist – we have seen the transformation in our peers. But still we have a suspicion that somehow this power might be unreachable or unattainable in our own lives. However, the story with Jesus didn't end with that man's comments. Jesus cured that boy and made him whole. Just as the Christian God is willing to work miracles when his believers are quite nearly hopeless, we are able to seek Divine assistance from our own Goddesses and Gods.

Step 7 does demonstrate some major difference between Christian and Pagan thought and history. One of the problems that Pagans have is also one of our more liberating benefits. The problem is the lack of an authoritative text. Christians are able to read and to believe specific acts that have been performed, by their God, on their behalf. They are able to take on faith that these works are accurate and true. As Pagans, we don't have that. In a sense, we need to trust in ourselves and in Deity even more than does the Christian.

Another difference between Christians and Pagans revolves around the nature of sin. In Christian reasoning, our defects are simply evils that may be plucked out from an individual by God. They are blemishes to be dissolved; malignancies, tumors and defects to be extracted. In the story above, the boy was plagued by demons and Christ healed the boy by exorcising those demons. However, we realize that what the Christian calls a defect is really nothing but the other side of something that is necessary; it is a much-needed part of our self that has, for whatever reason, been permitted to run amok. So rather than asking to have those defects simply removed, we seek the transformative power of deity to bring these "defects" back to their right use; to transform our weaknesses as RuneWolf would say.

We also see once again, that word "humble", and hopefully, at this point in our recovery, we have come to an understanding of humility which does not leave us confusing true humility with that self-effacing sort of false humility that is suggested by much of popular culture. We understand that humility does not imply a lack of strength, and we know that Deity will not simply lift most challenges from us. We will need to work quite hard, perhaps as hard as we've worked on anything prior to this point, but we will be given the strength to accomplish any transformation that we are willing to work for.

We can look to the Gods and Goddesses for examples of humility. The stories of the Gods are replete with tales of greatness and sacrifice. Self-sacrifice is the ultimate expression of humility because it places great value on something other than the individual. There is a story of how Odin hung upon a tree for nine days, wounded with a spear, without food or drink, as a sacrifice in order to obtain the Runes. He felt that the wisdom of the runes was worth the sacrifice. Humility is the honest recognition of what we possess within us, as well as what we do not. Odin, seeking greater wisdom, demonstrated such humility by recognizing that there was something he desired – some improvement within him – that was worthy of suffering.

We also recall the Charge of the Goddess at this point, when the Goddess said "If that which thou seekest, thou findest not within thee, thou wilt never find it without ..."[1], and know that while the assistance to change our lives exists, that the willingness, and the power to overcome the inertia of stillness exist within us alone. We need to open our mouths, to ask; we need to know that change is afoot, we need the will to change, and we need to dare to act according to that change. The Goddesses and the Gods will not change us without our cooperation, but they will act with our cooperation to help us achieve more than we could ever hope to manage through our own strength and will alone.

## Step 7 Practical Application

In Step 5, when we admitted our wrongs to our higher power, we opened our ears as well as our mouths. We didn't simply read a laundry list of defects to our particular Goddess or God, but we strove for some sort of dialogue. If we did listen, and if we wrote the words that were spoken to us, we may have some clues as to how we might begin to achieve this transformation we are seeking. Even if we didn't, it's likely that we've come to a new understanding of prayer and meditation by the time we've achieved this step. If so, then we can spend time in quiet meditation and ask, once again for this insight. If not, then this is a good time to seek that understanding. The ultimate goal of these steps is a spiritual transformation, and such transformations do not come about without an understanding of prayer and meditation.

Step 7, from a Pagan perspective, is not a passive experience. We have finally come to the point where our lives are now meaningful to us in a far deeper sense than ever before, and likely to those around us as well. Many people, when they have reached Step 7, are realizing that they are being asked to take on more responsibilities than they had in quite some time. Our changes are becoming evident to those around us as well. We are now at a point in our lives where action is required in both our personal and our spiritual lives.

It's time to now accept the responsibility that comes with the recognition being given us by our peers, and to begin to transform all the areas of our lives that are in need of change. Where before we had been unreliable, late or absent from work, we are now showing up on a regular basis. Our children no longer wonder if we'll pick them up from school, or worry about what mood we might be in when, and if we arrive. But these are all things that are expected and required from any nominally functional member of society. In Step 7, we begin to change; no longer to be merely nominally functional, but to be able to exhibit in our own lives the characteristics that we so admire in those individuals we consider extraordinary: the charity of Mother Theresa, the courage of Gandhi, the legendary truthfulness of George Washington. We may not achieve in this life the levels of those we so admire, but we can begin to walk those roads. We can model that type of behavior for those around us – for our neighbors, for our children, and we can begin to "be the change we wish to see in the world."[2]

# Step 7 Ritual

This, as are all rituals in this book, is meant as a starting point. These are suggestions, and you are free to modify whatever you see here as you wish. Because fire is involved in this ritual, weather, where you live, local codes and other circumstances may dictate that you adapt this ritual a bit. This particular ritual was the one that I used some years ago, and I did it out of doors in a forested area. If you choose to do the same, please be careful with the burning paper, and take measures to insure that no bits of smoldering paper will fly out of your control and start a fire. If you do decide to perform this ritual outside with fire, please be sure to bring a fire extinguisher or sufficient water to put out any fire that might be sparked. Be sure to clear any brush from the area before you start a fire, and don't do this particular ritual on a very dry or windy day.

To perform this ritual, you will need some paper (parchment paper is best, but other heavy paper such as card stock will work well), a small cauldron (something that will not burn or melt), a glass bowl or other container, a pen, a candle, matches, a small shovel or garden tool, and possibly a stone surface on which to work. You should have an outdoor place to work – somewhere that is open to the sky. You will be watching the smoke that you create for this ritual, and it is important to see it rise up and dissipate. The ritual may be done inside, but be sure that a window is open, that you won't be setting off any smoke alarms.

First, on a piece of parchment (or whatever type of paper you have chosen), write down each of the weaknesses you have identified in yourself during the inventory conducted in Step 4, leaving room to tear each one individually from that parchment. Once you have completed your list, tear out each item from the parchment (or cut them out with scissors if that's easier for you), and put them in the small bowl.

Light the small candle, and if it will not remain lighted due to a breeze, place it inside the cauldron. (If it's too breezy even for that, then it's probably too breezy to perform this ritual out-doors, and perhaps you should wait for some less windy day.) Now, one by one, take the individual pieces of parchment from the bowl and look at the character trait or "defect", and imagine what useful purpose it serves. For example, eating too much – what was listed among the Seven Deadly Sins as gluttony. We all have a need for food, and it is instinct to make sure that we have enough. At times, we may have gone longer than we should have without a decent meal. As children, especially if we grew up in a poor family, perhaps rather than having regular healthy snacks, we may have only had one or two real meals per day. For some of us, even that might have been a luxury! Perhaps our body still remembers childhood hunger, and rather than eating healthy portions during meals, with healthy snacks between, we eat more than our fair share. Concentrate on the fact that your body is still trying to take care of itself, but needs to re-learn some mechanism that will help you to eat in a more healthy fashion. Then, take the parchment with those words, and light it with the candle. Hold it in your fingers for as long as it is safe, watching it burn. (Hint: If you hold it to the side or with the paper above your fingers, you will be able to do so longer. Holding it facing down, with your fingers above will help it burn faster.) When it is almost burned away, place the remainder in your fire-safe cauldron. As you watch the paper transform into ash and smoke, visualize your "defect" also transforming into its more healthy alternative. The magick here is potent – we are using the transformation of physical objects into energy and another physical form to help us transform our character.

At the end of the ritual, once you have burned each piece of paper and you are certain that nothing is left smoldering, take your garden tool or small shovel and dig a small hole near a tree in which to bury the ashes from your ritual. If you performed this ritual in your home, maybe you can place the ashes with in the soil of some potted plant you have. Perhaps you might get a new plant that will live for some time. If you can, try to remember the location where you bury these ashes, and visit it every now and again during your sobriety to see how it has changed, and reflect on the changes in your own life. Change is one of the constants in all of our lives – nothing ever remains the same. Even from day to day, a great deal of change takes place whether it's detectable to our eyes or not. Our choice, with regard to change, is whether we will direct that change or simply permit it to happen to us. With ritual, we are directing, we are choosing, we are initiating, and that is a much better way to approach our lives.

Being passive, as many of us are, suggests that we have given up – that our life is less than important to us. It is a symptom of the disease process that we are trying to cure in the here and now. Those of us who used substances in the past can well remember the days, when high or drunk or somehow or other in an altered state, we had our dreams of grandeur in which we were the top dogs with the world at our feet. Or, as a co-dependent, perhaps we had dreams of how we would change our loved one, to fix what was wrong. But in the end it was all a passive endeavor, and we really never dealt with the true essence of our difficulties, which was always within us.

Magick is not a passive endeavor – it requires tremendous focus and energy. It is an active force designed to bring about real effects. When we learn magick, we learn transformative techniques, and strangely enough we discover that the true secret to changing the world comes from changing the way we view the world. The true secret of changing our self is in changing the way we see our self. The true secret to changing another person is to change the way we see that other person. And the most important secret, after all the transformation in our self, is to recognize what we have power to change and to accept the rest as exactly how it is supposed to be.

[1] Doreen Valiente, The Charge of the Goddess

[2] Mahatma Ghandi

# Step 8

### *Made a list of all persons we had harmed and became willing to make amends to them all.*

How can we come to know all of the people we may have harmed? Many of us will have completed some sort of list when we worked through Step 4; others of us will have merely compiled a list of traits that we know need to be changed. There will be some difference in Step 8 which depends on how we did the previous steps, but the real focus in Step 8 isn't the simple task of accounting – it's in recognizing what we have done to others, achieving some level of empathy toward them, and becoming willing to do something about it.

The difficulties that we have caused some individuals are blatantly obvious: if we've stolen from them, if we assaulted them, if we cheated on our spouse or padded expense accounts; each of these things is an obvious wrong. Anyone who has suffered some sort of addiction has likely fallen short of Asatru's Nine Noble Virtues of Courage, Truth, Honor, Fidelity, Discipline, Hospitality, Industriousness, Self-Reliance, and Perseverance. We who have suffered addiction have likely caused unnecessary harm to others and have shown little regard for the Wiccan Rede.

Pagans typically claim to have a reverence for Nature; might not Nature be included in the list of those we may have harmed? What of ourselves? If we have spent years living in a state of defeat, having become subservient to the obsession of drugs or alcohol, we have certainly harmed ourselves. If we have been the enablers, even unwittingly, of another person's habits – does that warrant some sort of amends? If we are dedicated to a particular goddess or god, might we also offer them some sort of amends?

Most of us, when new to sobriety, may feel that we've really caused little harm to others. We might imagine that because we were still able to pay our bills, to care for our children, to make it to work on time and work all the hours that were required of us, to nominally fulfill what was required of us, we had really caused harm to none but ourselves. But upon completing Step 4, we should have a much better idea of the wreckage we've left in our wake. We may be getting an idea that a passing ship may not collide with another, but it can leave behind a wake that impacts everything around it. A ship too close to shore or moving too quickly can cause damage to smaller vessels moored nearby. While we were in the midst of our illness, we may have been like that ship, moving at full-speed, oblivious to the damage that was being left in our wake.

Now having discovered sobriety and having committed to changing our lives, we are faced with the difficult task of taking ownership and responsibility for the damage we have left behind us. The temptation is great to "let sleeping dogs lie" – to move ahead with our new lives and not to bring up the past. While we've admitted our wrongdoings to our self, to Deity, and to another human being, we are faced presently with a task that seems far more difficult – that of being honest to those whom we have wronged.

However, the wisdom that is built into each of these steps is remarkable. This step involves "making a list of those we harmed", and becoming willing to make such amends as may be due. We can rest and take a breath and recognize that we aren't just to go out and approach each and everyone we've harmed, right now. The task at hand is to become willing, to prepare ourselves, to create a plan. We can remember back to our ritual of willingness in which we recognized that each and every task we perform, each movement, each conscious thought is preceded by an act of willingness – and that willingness itself may be preceded by an act of will. Having been diligent thus far, we may be noticing something interesting about these steps. They never urge us to action without the preparation necessary to insure that action will bring about satisfactory results; they never call us to do something that will place us in a state of peril or danger. Before any course of action is undertaken, we have thought about it and prepared for it. Unlike those days in the midst of our illness, we don't simply do or act – we think, we prepare, we plan, we become willing, and then, when all is in place, we execute our plan. And right now, we are planning and working toward making direct amends to those whom we have caused harm by whatever addictive behavior it was that we had engaged in.

It might make sense at this point to consider our motives for putting particular individuals on the list, and to consider just how we will make these amends. If we consider our motives, it will go much easier for us when it comes time to address each instance. Any of us can have selfish or selfless motives. If our motives are selfish, if our purpose for making amends is to "show them we've changed, and that now, we are deserving of their respect", then we're not really ready to make amends. We're simply seeking our own gratification – and that is a behavior we've already engaged in many times in the past. Becoming willing to make amends involves an act of selflessness and being ready to accept the consequences for what we've done. There is more than a fair chance that our attempts at making amends with certain people will result in harsh words from them. They might rebuff our efforts, they might greet us with anger when they see us, and we might find that we're met with doors shut in our faces. Will we be ready for this? Are we prepared to face such situations with calmness and acceptance? Are we ready to recognize the justness of the other individual's position, and to accept their words with dignity and with respect?

And what of the amends we may owe nature? How can we possibly offer amends to the Earth? In what ways might we have harmed her? In what ways might our using have offended her? I don't know about anyone else, but when my mind wasn't working properly, I was fairly destructive and wasteful; that's certainly one sort of offense. Even if I thought I was environmentally conscious when using, might such using have had an effect on the environment? How many acres of woodland and rainforest are used today for growing illegal drugs; how many acres are simply burned to make way for providing us with more marijuana, cocaine, and opium? Don't we actually contribute to deforestation when we use? How many parties might we have attended in the woods and secluded areas, leaving messes and broken bottles and the like? Consuming a case per day of beer, are we really considering recycling? What about our cigarettes ... how many butts actually make it into a proper receptacle, compared to the number we toss on the ground? Have we really been driving a vehicle that is environmentally sound, or have we ignored oil leaks, poor mileage and the like because we had "better" things to spend our money on?

The point of this step isn't to beat ourselves up, but it's to become willing to look at us and our relationships honestly, and to become willing to take responsibility for our actions or our inaction, and to do better in the future. We aren't to become morose, but to be honest and responsible people, part of a community, and to live with integrity, recognizing when we have harmed another and to act promptly when we have. By becoming willing to make amends to each of those we have harmed in the past, we are setting as well a pattern for the future; no longer will we be the foolish one who upon breaking something in someone's home or shop, will stand there in front of the evidence and say "It wasn't me."

## Step 8 Practical Application

When we have reached Step 8, we are finally beginning to see just how much our personal behavior is able to affect the lives of those around us – positively or negatively. "No man is an island," and as such, each and every action we take influences the lives of those around us. We may have heard of the butterfly effect, which suggests that the breeze or the turbulence of the wings of a butterfly, while having a small effect on the local environment, could have dramatic consequences in the future. Chaos theory suggests that a very small change in initial conditions can have a remarkable dynamic effect in the future. Some people say that the effects of alcoholism or addiction can influence our families for a number of generations.

It is in Step 8 that we become willing to see how much of an effect we have had on our environment – of family, friends, co-workers, neighbors and all those we have touched in our lives. Also, here we then become willing to make whatever amends are due each of them.

In Step 8, we are developing traits of character that will serve us throughout the rest of our lives – we are further developing our integrity, and we are developing the capacity to be responsible for our actions. When we have this capacity to see where and when we have harmed another, we can begin to develop another, very useful skill – to think ahead. As addicts and alcoholics and enablers – each of us has been acting out of reaction or control, but always with the intent of making our own life easier to live. Having been faced with our own seemingly insurmountable difficulties, we now see that the solution for our personal lives may have made life exceptionally difficult for others. In looking at this – in going through the process of seeing exactly how our choices have been injurious to others, we have a tool that is of almost incalculable value – we can see, with the lens of the past, how our actions in the future might affect others. Not only are we able to see how we *have* harmed others – we are able to predict how our current actions *might* harm others in the future, and more importantly – we can avoid any such action in the future. Having had the opportunity to see how our actions have affected the lives of others is the pearl of great price that we have found in the wreckage of our past. The price has been paid, in part, by others – and in Step 8, we become willing, through the offering of amends to those who have already paid their share, to step up and pay our own arrears.

## Step 8 Ritual

Our ritual in Step 8 is one in which we seek clearer vision to know who it is that we have harmed in our past and to see what damage has been left in our wake. We naturally want to know how far that damage extends, because this knowledge will help us to know what might be required to right such wrongs.

We're all familiar with family trees. They can be depicted in a number of ways, but one popular way to draw them places us at the center, with our family radiating about us in a great circle. The closer we are to the center of our circle, the closer we are to our selves; as we move farther out toward the more distant leaves we move back in time.

We can also construct a tree of influence. This is like a family tree, but instead of moving back in time, we move outward in our relations. In our inner circle, we have our self. Moving out is our immediate family, consisting of us, our spouse, our children – those who live in the same home as us. Then we might have our parents, brothers and sisters and possibly our friends and co-workers, or fellow students if we're still in school. Moving out to increasingly distant levels, we might have cousins, grandparents, the families of our friends, schoolmates or co-workers.

What we will do in this ritual is to get a large piece of paper and construct such a tree of influence. If you can find a white paper table cloth, that will work well – or perhaps a sheet of news print or craft paper. Whatever sort of paper that it is that you use, it should be a single piece of paper, or failing that, a number of sheets that will remain connected together.

You will also need some sort of container large enough to fit your final work into – a large basin, your bathtub, plastic sandbox, etc. (If you can't find a container large enough, then a piece of plastic large enough to place the paper in, on level ground with the edges of the plastic raised, will also work.) You will also need some water-soluble ink, dye, or food coloring.

After spending some time in meditation looking for where in your life you may have harmed another, begin to create your circle with a pen, pencil or marker. Place yourself in the center and then move outward until you can think of all those who you may have directly influenced in your life. This may take a great deal of time. You aren't here thinking of how you may have harmed people – just those you have influenced, those who you have had contact with. Nor is accuracy important here – if a person should have been in an inner circle and you think of them later, just put them where you can.

When the circle is complete, look at it and see how many lives you have influenced just by being here on this Earth. Recognize also that this circle is likely incomplete – we know few of the people on the road with us when we drive, those on an airplane when we fly, but we touch many, many lives. However, for our purpose here this circle is complete. Next we fill whatever vessel it is that we have, part way – perhaps an inch, with water, and gently lay our circle on that water so that it's resting on the surface.

Now we take our ink and drop one drop in the center. Watch that ink spread over the paper – see how far it goes. Did one drop affect just us? Add a second drop and see how much further it goes – then a few more drops. You'll see that it doesn't take many drops to affect almost everyone on our list. Let the paper remain on or in the water for the next hour or so and see how far that circle of ink spreads. Recognize that your actions are like that ink for good or for ill, and that each and every action you take impacts first the people close to you, and then spreads outward, as did the ink.

Our addictions or enabling behavior are like these drops – each time that we engage in whatever it was that we're seeking recovery from was one more drop that rippled outward through our own sphere of influence. Like our paper here, the entirety of that sphere has been stained by our own actions. Let's say that one night we were out using a substance. We might assume that because we weren't home, we weren't acting badly to our husband, our wife, our children. But they likely know where we are, or what we are doing – they know why we aren't home when they expected. And their moods, because of our actions are affected. And as they interact with others, their moods affect those interactions. And our behavior has rippling effects through our community, through our families, our friends and beyond.

Cleaning up, we can let that water drain, and let the paper dry. If you wish, you can dispose of it as you move on to Step 9, or you can keep it as a reminder, and dispose of it later. If and when you do dispose of it, treat it with the respect that you would with any ritual item – burning, burial and other such methods are ideal. Some people have a clay jar or pot which they use for such things, and when it is full, the jar and its contents are buried. How you do things is certainly up to you, but it also says something about you. What do you wish your ritual items to say about you?

## Step 9

*Made direct amends to such people wherever possible,*
*except when to do so would injure them or others.*

Almost everyone who engages in a Twelve Step program of recovery approaches Step 9 with some degree of trepidation. Every other step involves working on our selves or with Deity. Even in Step 5, where we admitted our shortcomings to another human being, we were free to choose that person in whom we confided. Here in Step 9 we're charged with the task of meeting individuals to whom we have caused some harm, face-to-face, and admitting our wrongs, our misdeeds. It can be quite a daunting task; it's a challenge that's not for the faint of heart. Just prior to my own undertaking of Step 9, though, someone came up to me and asked who I was. They then told me that they owed me an amends for something that had happened many years ago, and I recognized this person as someone who I went to school with. I actually had no recollection of the incident of which he spoke, and was quite happy that he could feel better about things. It was at this point that I started to gain just a bit of understanding of what Step 9 is all about.

Looking back at the times I've wronged people, and comparing these situations to the times when I've been wronged, I noticed a pattern: when someone has wronged me, for the most part, I've been willing to forgive. I recognize that we're all human, and that we do, on occasion, hurt others simply by not thinking, by being occasionally selfish, but not as often out of sheer malice. For those times when people have wronged me due to actions stemming from simple human frailties, I rarely harbor any resentment. I might learn to keep from being taken advantage of, but I don't typically entertain and nourish feelings of ill-will toward anybody.

On the other hand, when I've wronged another, those feelings linger. I might feel guilty and stay away from the people that I've harmed, not wanting to face them because I suspect they'll still be angry, or because I have no way to offer recompense for the things I've done. These feelings remain long after the event may have been forgotten by the individual I have wronged ... they stay and fester within me as a poison with no outlet.

Step 9 is our opportunity to lance the boils, the festering wounds of guilt, to remove the poison within us that is keeping us from repairing those relationships with our relatives, loved ones and co-workers. It's not an easy task; it can be difficult to approach those we may have borrowed money from but not yet repaid, those we may have stolen from, those we may have lied to, a lover we may have cheated on ... here we face our own basest humanity in its raw nakedness. It is not about going to people with excuses and we aren't to blame our behavior on external influences; the fact that we were high or intoxicated or addicted does not absolve us of taking responsibility for our actions. We have already admitted our misdeeds, we have already identified those to whom amends are owed. Step 9 is simply about our own accountability for those things we done, and doing what we can to make right the relationships that were damaged as a result of our actions, or our inaction.

Having the list that we created in step 8, it's time to look through that list and to determine to whom and when we will begin to make those amends. It might be, and quite probably will be that some of these people are very close to us, and we can begin right away. But before we rush headlong into the task of ridding our souls of the guilt we carry, we need to look at the second phase of Step 9 – "except when to do so would injure them or others." Here our desire for absolution can be at odds with the reality of a situation. We need to consider the possibility that revealing certain events to certain individuals might in fact be injurious. Take, for example, an affair we might have had with the husband or wife of a co-worker; should we tell our partner? Suppose that we're married and we reveal the fact that we had a fling to someone else who is married. If we reveal that to our partner, will they possibly reveal that information to the other couple? If they do, will that cause harm to them? Our partner, should we wish to not reveal with whom we had that affair might demand that information from us, offer an ultimatum to reveal who it was, divorce us, and break up the family ... and the fallout of such a revelation could be drastic. Yet still, we wish to be free from the guilt of the situation.

Here, the Wiccan Rede reminds us "An it harm none, do what thou wilt. It seems to fall right in line with Step 9. There are times when what we have done is a very heavy burden simply because there is no easy way to rid our selves of it – nor is there any way to lighten the load. There may be actions we have taken which, if revealed, will cause great harm to a number of people. In these rare cases, there is no one to who we can reveal what we've done, and we might be saddled with the sad duty of holding on to that information, our only amends being to live our lives with dignity and to avoid such traps in the future.

Step 9 does not promise us that we will be free from the guilt; it merely offers us the opportunity to clean up our side of the street by making amends. It might well be that our amends to another might not involve any sort of absolution; it might be that our amends takes the form of truly turning over a new leaf, living in a different fashion. We can't jeopardize the well-being or the happiness of another so that we can put a salve on our own wounds. However, we also can't let ourselves live in a fantasy that suggests that any revelation of our wrongs will certainly cause harm to another. We can't hide behind a fabricated suspicion of possible injury in order to utilize what we perceive as an easy way out.

When we do begin to make our amends, it's perhaps easiest to do so with those who know something of our situation, who know that we're in recovery, and who understand that we are actively working to change our lives. These people know our history, they have probably been encouraging us and supporting us through the entire process; they may have even been the ones who urged us to seek help in the first place. It's doubtful that we've never wronged people such as this, and they can be very helpful to us as we take our first steps on the road to learning how to be accountable for our actions.

Before we approach anyone, though, we need to know exactly what it is that we are doing and what we have to offer by way of amends. Were not only admitting our faults, or how we might have harmed or injured another, but we're seeking to make right the situation. When we approach someone, perhaps someone whom we might have forgot to repay after they loaned us a sum of money, it is of little help to them to say simply "I know I borrowed that money, and I'm sorry I never repaid you." That leaves them in the exact position they were in before we came to them, except that they realize we do now understand that we still owe the money. We need to recognize for ourselves exactly how we might have wronged another, and to have a plan to properly settle accounts. At this stage in our recovery, it's quite possible that we are now employed again, if we had lost our jobs. Or if we never lost our jobs, it's entirely likely that we're no longer spending large sums of money on booze, sex, or drugs, and that we are better off financially. Here, when we approach an individual we owe money to, we can work out a way to repay them what we owe them, even if it's a small amount of money at a time. Some people might forgive our debts, and we should bear this in mind when we find ourselves being owed money from another ... passing on favors such as this not only blesses another, but it is good karma as well, not to mention the feeling that both the lender and debtor have when generosity is practiced.

Step 9 is not a practice that one goes about for a day or two, or even a number of months; it can take years, possibly the rest of our lives. However, working to be responsible builds a great deal of character, and it will be the one tool that will serve to make us respectable people in our societies. It is a symbol of both humility and integrity, for there are few if any of us who do no wrong. Those of us who can admit our faults and seek to change the nature that brings about those faults are people who are working to be trustworthy.

## Step 9 Practical Application

The one quality that is necessary to accomplish Step 9 is courage. Courage, to many, is equivalent to fearlessness, but nothing could be further from the truth. If there is no fear, courage is unnecessary – it takes no courage to accomplish a thing where one does not feel danger or threat. Quite to the contrary, fearlessness in the face of danger is foolhardiness. One needs only look at the 0 card in the Tarot – the Fool. This is a foolhardy character, blithely unaware of the precarious position he is in as he strolls along the cliff's edge.

Courage acknowledges fear, but acts nonetheless in the way which will bring about what is the desired outcome despite that fear. It acknowledges danger or threat, and then continues to do what is necessary. Without this trait, Step 9 cannot be fulfilled.

When we live our lives, there are many times when courage is necessary – we know what the right and proper course of action is, but we are faced with a paralyzing fear that often prevents us from taking that action. Step 9 and its fulfillment will teach us that we can find within us that courage to do what is necessary and right, despite the perilous nature of the circumstance.

When we first approach Step 9, we will be faced with many people who are owed some sort of amends from us. Some we may have harmed deeply; others only mildly. Some of these people may be our friends still, and others may have long since ended any relationship with us. If we are not yet people of courage, diving directly into the deep end of the pool isn't always the wisest way to increase our courage. Often it's best to take much smaller steps.

If acting courageously is new to us, then we might start, not by going to those we suspect will greet us with acrimony, but rather to someone who we suspect will be understanding – someone who has seen our struggles and recognizes that we are changing. Some might think this is taking the easy road, but in reality it's merely the first step on a much longer road. The first steps when climbing a mountain aren't done on a cliff, halfway up the mountain. Rather, we begin at the base. Even on large mountains, base camp is the first goal.

Likewise, with Step 9, we needn't begin with the biggest challenges first – we can start small, and take the larger or more difficult steps later. This doesn't mean that we avoid large steps altogether – the goal is to climb the mountain, not to look as if we are trying to climb the mountain. It makes little sense to begin a journey that we have no intention of completing.

As we work on Step 9, most of us eventually encounter someone who rebuffs our attempts at making amends. Most of us are acquainted with one or more people who have witnessed our repeated promises of living sober, someone whom we have hurt so badly that they no longer wish to see us, or someone whose trust we have so abused that they can no longer risk trusting us. These are times to summon up both courage and humility. We need the humility to recognize that no matter how far we come, no matter how long we work this program, there may be some who will never wish to be in our company again.

To be effective in Step 9, we must be willing to encounter these situations head-on. We must respond without anger, and we must be willing to respect the wishes of those who express such desires. This can be heart-wrenching, but we must accept this as a consequence of our past actions.

For those who no longer wish to be in our company, or those who cannot – perhaps due to death or distance – amends must take the form of "living amends", recompense for our prior actions by changing our present lives. Perhaps we owe a company financial amends; perhaps they fired us because of our bad behavior, but have chosen to not to file charges. But the owner no longer wishes to see us – they don't want, or won't accept anything from us. This might leave us feeling guilty (and perhaps it should), but we can still make an amend of sorts. We can take what was owed that individual or business and make a donation to a worthy group or cause. We might offer prayers for those who no longer wish to be with us, praying only for their well-being and happiness. We can volunteer for organizations pledging a certain amount of time for debts owed that we can no longer repay. This can be difficult, but it does build our character.

When we have met the challenges of Step 9, we will discover that our personal character traits of courage, humility and dedication have improved a great deal. We will learn that there is likely no task that will be too daunting for us. We will recognize that we can play as a part of a team because the desire to be the big-shot has left us.

## Step 9 Ritual

Prior to engaging in battle, our ancestors had many rituals which offered them strength and helped them to summon courage. There were rites which would help their weapons to strike true, their armor to stay secure, and other rituals designed to thwart the efforts of the enemy. While Step 9 is not concerned with warfare and we aren't concerned with deflecting missiles from enemy combatants, we are doing something that is very difficult and which in a reasonable person does call up feelings of fear and trepidation.

There are many rituals that can help at these times – firewalking would certainly be one such. If there is such an event scheduled nearby, by all means, attend it – you will discover something within you that you likely didn't know existed. But we don't always have access to a firewalking ritual right when we need one, and our ancestors did have other techniques to help summon courage. Here we're going to create an amulet.

Amulets have been used for many millennia to help the bearer maintain courage while performing difficult tasks. We can make an amulet to help us discover courage. Its worthy to note that Aquamarine is said to be a stone for courage. It's also the same color as the throat Chakra, and what we'll be doing as we make amends is speaking. The Aquamarine will thus comprise at least part of our amulet of courage.

There are a number of ways of creating amulets, and what method you choose will be up to you. One way is to simply use the stone as a necklace; you can find springy bead cages for semi-precious stones – simply place your Aquamarine inside one of these cages, attach a chain or cord, and you have a piece of jewelry. This is especially appropriate because, as a necklace, the stone associated with the throat chakra is placed where it should be.

You can also place a piece of Aquamarine inside a small bag – a mojo bag, perhaps with other items that speak to courage – a shark's tooth, a feather from a bird of prey, a bear claw. There are also herbs that are associated with courage – Black Cohosh, Marjoram and others are known for this property. You might also consider the lowly Dandelion, as its name comes to us from the French and means "teeth of a lion". You might also find an Aquamarine ring or other jewelry that you could wear or carry.

When you have decided what your amulet will consist of, gather up the components and either at Sunrise, or at night during a waxing moon, you can perform this ritual. The Sunrise is often a good time for this sort of magic because the Sun has been associated with strength. A waxing moon is appropriate for bringing things toward us, such as courage.

You will need some spring water and salt, a shallow bowl, a clean face-towel or cloth that will be used only for ritual purposes. (In fact, tools that are used for ritual purposes should be used only for ritual purposes, with the possible exception of kitchen implements as used by kitchen witches – but then again, ask any two Pagans their opinion on this and you're bound to get at least three answers. Still, I don't like using ritual items for mundane purposes.)

Be sure that you will be able to see the Sun or the Moon from where you are. Ground and center yourself and meditate on the difficult task (Step 9 in this case) that you are faced with. When you are ready and the Sun or Moon is visible, place the Aquamarine in the bowl with a little salt. Salt is purifying. Then pour the water over the stone and into the bowl. If you have a Mojo bag with herbs or other items that are part of your amulet, you can place them around the bowl.

Position yourself so that you are able to see the stone in the bowl, and the reflection of the Sun or the Moon in that same bowl. Visualize the heavenly body filling the stone (and any other parts of your amulet that might be around the bowl) with energy that will sustain you as you go about your difficult task. Visualize yourself as you speak with both confidence and sincere repentance for what you have done to harm another. Visualize the fact that you have the ability to make proper amends for whatever may have happened. Continue this visualization until the Sun or the Moon is no longer reflected in the bowl, and then remove the stone and dry it with the cloth or towel. Assemble your amulet and wear it as you complete Step 9. You might find that it will help to wear it whenever you encounter a difficult task, especially one that requires communication.

# Step 10

*Continued to take personal inventory and when we
were wrong promptly admitted it.*

If we're working the steps diligently, we might begin to
recognize that despite our attempts at personal growth and
improvement, there are still aspects of our lives that we aren't
satisfied with – we still act in ways that don't reflect our highest will
for our lives. Some of us recognize that we are still acting in ways
that leave us less than proud of what we've done. Our work in the
previous six steps has helped us to recognize our faults, and we
might still be working to transform them through new behavior,
and we're committed to a more spiritual path, but at times we still
slip unthinkingly into old habits and behaviors. Step 10 is our
opportunity to nip such ingrained reactions in the bud. Some
people think of this as a sort of mini-step 4, others call it a spot-
check inventory, but however you look at it, it is a tool that we can
use to continuously evaluate ourselves. This is important because
without knowing where we are, right now, it's difficult to decide in
what direction we need to go to keep our growth constant.

As we continue to evolve it's important to keep in mind the
work we've done so far, and to avoid destructive coping
mechanisms and habits that we know have failed us in the past. In
the previous steps we've worked to change our thinking, and now
is our opportunity to put those changes into practice. We'll
regularly take stock of what we've done and do what we can to
make things right as soon as possible.

This continuing personal inventory is not the same exhaustive
survey of our lives that we completed in Step 4. It does not need to
be a formal exercise that we do with pen and paper, though some
people who journal are inclined to take stock while doing so. The
methods of taking such an inventory are many, but they all serve
the common goal of keeping us aware of exactly who and what we
are.

Step 10 also reminds us continuously to remain true to our
ideals. A process of continuous self-appraisal and admission of our
faults gives us continuous reinforcement to improve our
relationships with others. It teaches us that this sort of
reinforcement doesn't have to come from without; we don't need
some external taskmaster to keep us on track – we can do this on
our own. We are no longer children in need of parenting, we don't
require something or someone outside of our self, telling us

whether what we have just done is good or bad – instead, we are now adults, and know whether or not what we did was right. We are able, as adults, to evaluate each of our actions, and to discern for ourselves the consequence of those actions – in our lives and in the lives of those affected. The personal requirement to admit our wrongdoings, especially to those we wrong, can be an inducement to choose right action rather than wrong.

In the past sometimes we found it exciting to do wrong, or being part of a group that was doing something wrong. For many of us, petty theft – shoplifting small items, speeding, taking advantage of obvious errors at a bank or checkout line or an obviously incorrectly priced item at a box store – all of these things have been exciting opportunities for us. We knew that we were either doing something that was obviously and objectively wrong, but it felt good to get away with it. Sooner or later, though, we will find that doing wrong no longer holds the same excitement or fascination that it once may have, and this is a real and tangible sign that we are growing in our behavior and in our spirituality.

# Step 10 Practical Application

Step 10 can provide each of us with many practical benefits that might not at first be obvious. How many of us spend hours in bed, trying to go to sleep because we can't let go of the worries of the day? We may be troubled by what we've done, how we reacted to something someone else has done, or we might be worried about things that are coming tomorrow as a direct result of what we may have done yesterday. If we are engaged in a method of constant self-appraisal, we are far more than one step ahead – we can go to bed at night knowing that we have done what we could do throughout the day, either to act with righteousness or to correct any unrighteousness. It is easier to leave the troubles and worries of the day behind when we are able to recognize that we have done and dealt with everything we are capable of, and that it's now time to sleep.

At this point we have also learned that "legal" and "righteous" are two very different words with different and not necessarily reconcilable meanings. What is legal may not always be righteous, and what is righteous may not necessarily be legal. Take the case of that incorrectly priced item at our box store. It may be legal to try to take advantage of a price tag that's wrong – some states require a store to sell an item for the price on the package. But is it right or proper to take advantage of an obvious error? Because we find a 52" High def OLED television priced at $125.00 instead of $1250.00 … while the law might require a store to sell it at that price because it was their error, is it righteous to take advantage of such an error? Or might it be better to point out the error? It's possible that the store would still be willing to sell it for that price, but the real question in our minds deals with intentions. Were we trying to take advantage of another's errors, or were we trying to do the right thing? We also need to bear in mind once again that all scores are settled at one time or another, and the less Karmic debt that we build up, the more accounts that we can properly settle on our own in the here and the now, the easier things will be to deal with in the future.

If, as many suggest, blood pressure and other health issues are related to stress, then Step 10 may be one of the most healthy activities that we can engage in. In continuously working Step 10 in our lives, we are cleaning up the dark corners and closets of our lives. The baggage that accompanies so many of us throughout our lives simply doesn't have the opportunity to sit there, to gather dust and be a constant irritation in our minds, and then make an untimely appearance at some point in the future. Instead, we are constantly clearing out that baggage and doing the mental house-cleaning that enables us to relax – knowing that we have nothing that is going to rear its ugly head and bite us.

It's been said, and we hear these words in many 12-Step programs, that we are only as sick as our secrets; while that may not be entirely true, the fact is that the more secrets we have, the more masks and alternate identities we will use to keep others from seeing who we truly are. Keeping secrets by their very nature causes us to lie, whether we like to admit it or not. Keeping secrets is a form of dishonesty, whether it be in a court of law or in our daily life. While sometimes a certain amount of dishonesty is acceptable – telling your aged grandmother that she can't cook as well as she once did is certainly not going to endear you to the rest of the family, nor will it be a comfort to your grandmother – the regular habit of keeping our own wrongdoings secret, rather than dealing with them and changing who we are, is simply counterproductive to living a better life.

The active part of Step 10 comes after we admit our wrongs. The process of admitting our wrongs urges us to do right. It's a process that is not so banal as simply causing us to recoil from bad action because we know that at some point the piper will have to be paid; rather, we are consistently reminded of who we are and who and what we honestly desire to be. This constant self-appraisal helps us to measure where we are and to compare that to what our highest will is for our self, and few motivational techniques are likely to surpass this as we try to gain personal integrity.

As typical human beings, we often have one common failing – when things aren't spelled out for us, we subscribe to the easiest possible interpretation of the challenge before us. We might look at "continued to take personal inventory" and recognize that there is no specific timeframe suggested. Should we take that inventory hourly? Daily? Weekly? Monthly? While the step offers no specific time period, many people working these steps have offered their own suggestions. Perhaps the most common of these is daily – each night prior to sleep, as mentioned above, is quite common. Others continuously take their own inventory, choosing to be rid of an issue as soon as it appears. Some take yearly retreats in which they take a more formal inventory as they did in Step 4, but still they work to recognize when they are wrong and deal with those situations immediately. There is certainly no single technique that will be sufficient for every one of us – we are all different, we have different priorities, different journeys, and a dogmatic approach to anything is pretty much anathema to modern Pagans. But the spiritual principle of constant self-appraisal is something that is useful to us all. The job for each of us is to find a means to achieve that – whether it's a daily practice or a weekly ritual or constant mindfulness. Each of us will find the technique that works best for us, and the best technique is the one that we will consistently use.

## Step 10 Ritual

(Note: This ritual should not be attempted by people whose addictive behaviors are related to food, by diabetics, or by others who may suffer physical problems without consulting health care providers first.)

The ritual for Step 10 has more than one goal: It tries to impress that there are things that we need to do continually on a day-to-day basis. We must do things consistently if we are to survive. If we stopped breathing, for instance, our bodies would perish in mere moments. We also see that many things that we do for our selves can be quite good for us, or they can cause us harm, depending on how we perform them. Eating, as one example, is a necessary function. But eating the wrong things, or too much of something that is good, can cause us harm. Eating is a choice that we make daily; one which, if we ignore it, at first begins to cause us discomfort, and if we ignore it for too long, it begins to affect our health. For this reason, in our ritual for Step 10, we are going to make use of fasting in our ritual. If you have some sort of illness which requires you to avoid fasting, talk to your physician and see what level of fasting might be appropriate and safe. Many people, even with medical conditions, are able to do a one-day fast with slight modification.

To perform the ritual for Step 10, we'll need to set aside one day for the exercise. In the morning, begin the day with a shower and your usual morning routine, with the exception of breakfast. You may drink water. If you have a heavy caffeine habit, then a cup of coffee may be necessary to avoid withdrawals and the resulting headache. As you go throughout your day, notice how your body is reacting to being without food.

With each pang of hunger recognize that your body is making you increasingly aware that it doesn't have the raw materials to maintain itself normally and still accomplish the tasks asked of it. Normally we consume foods that are broken down into raw materials that can be used to produce energy, which allows us to move our limbs, to maintain body temperature, and to breathe, pump blood and maintain our mental functioning. On this day we aren't eating, so the raw materials to maintain those function come from our body's reserves. Instead of breaking down food, our body is likely reclaiming energy stored as fat. If there is insufficient fat, then the body will resort to reclaiming muscle, just to stay alive.

We need to eat to stay alive for any significant period of time. But there are other things that we require as well. If we don't maintain a healthy mental outlook, just as surely as we suffer from a lack of food, we will also suffer if we have negative attitudes. So with each pang of hunger, examine your life for the past week. Try to discern where your attitudes may have failed you over the past week. Recognize that as your body is struggling with the lack of nourishment, so does the mind suffer with lack of proper care. Tools such as reflection, forgiveness and a daily practice of integrity are the proper nourishment for spirit.

Most healthy people can survive for quite some time without food, but survival without water is not likely beyond a few days. There are some exceptions, such as the Indian Yogi Prahlad Jani[1] who claims not to have eaten food nor drunk water for some 70 years, but for most of us food and water are necessities.

Mentally healthy people – those who make a regular practice of reflecting on their actions, writing wrongs and resolving not to repeat past errors – might also survive for a time without such reflection. As you continue to experience hunger throughout the day, meditate on the fact that just as your body needs for you to do that which will sustain it, so does your mind and your spirit. Where the effects of not eating are hunger and declining physical health, the effects of not caring for the spirit are declining values, a loss of integrity, a reduced tolerance for uncomfortable or difficult situations, and, ultimately, a likelihood of relapse of the condition that brought us to the Twelve Step programs in the first place.

At the end of your fast in the evening, try to eat a light meal – if you try to make up for all the food you missed during the day, you'll probably overdo it. It's never a good idea to break a period of fasting with a large meal.

[1]http://abcnews.go.com/Health/International/man-eat-drink/story?id=10787036

# Step 11

> *Sought through prayer, meditation and our craft to improve our conscious contact with Deity, praying for knowledge and understanding of our own highest will, the Divine plan for us, and the power to carry that out.*

Any Pagan who has been through any serious program of study has certainly learned the value of meditation – it is fundamental to performing magick. But prayer has a much more difficult time of it in Pagan (especially Neo-Pagan) circles than in any of the monotheistic religions. Many of us view prayer with disdain, having come from patriarchal religions where one must submit to the will of God as delivered through some ecclesiastical hierarchy.

But prayer doesn't have to mean that sort of submission. In Paganism, rather than being ruled by Deity, some of us view the Gods and Goddesses as beings who are desiring of having a relationship with us, and with whom we can work on a cooperative basis. While we may have different creation myths, most Pagans recognize that Deity is not some distant, unapproachable entity who rules and uses Nature, but more an individual who expresses herself or himself through Nature, much as a dancer expresses themselves with their body and with their movements. Where in some religions God creates a world which man may subjugate and use, Paganism (at least many forms of it) views Nature as the body or the expression of the Divine and urges us to cooperate.

So prayer, from a Pagan perspective is not a submissive act which we must do, but a welcome and cooperative act in which we desire to commune with the Divine. Where in some religions one might seek to know God's will, and the strength to carry that out however unpleasant it might be, Paganism recognizes that our own highest will already knows what is best and seeks to have that expressed and made manifest on a physical level. In our communication with Deity through prayer, we seek the wisdom to achieve what it will take to make that come to pass.

Prayer, spells, and meditation are very similar and often confused, so let's look at what each of these is:

Prayer is communication with Deity. It can be in the form of a petition, in which we are asking for something. It can be intercessory, in which we ask for something on behalf of another. There are also prayers of praise and adoration, which are self-explanatory; there are prayers of penitence in which we express sorrow or regret for our sins; there are prayers of thanksgiving and even imprecatory prayer, which is similar to a curse in which we ask the Divine to injure, maim or to kill another person. Prayer can be one-way or two-way. For most people, prayer is simply one-way communication – many of us simply let our God(s) know what we want and hope that it will come to pass. You'll hear "God, if you get me out of this mess, I promise never to do that again", or "God, please let my loan for a new car (or truck or house or whatever) be approved." That's not usually the most productive form of prayer. Instead, what we're looking for is something more on the line of "Great Spirit, please speak to me; let me know where I went wrong, and how to fix it", followed by a period of silent reflection. It's a lot like going to a therapist – we can spend hours upon hours talking about how messed up our lives are, and it won't get us anywhere. But when we listen as well and heed suggestions offered, we have a chance of making some real and effective changes in the way we do things.

Spells are different than prayer because unlike prayer, they are designed to produce an actual result in the here and now, in accordance with our own efforts and desires. Spells may involve prayer, but the purpose is a specific and intended result. We might know someone who is in desperate need of a new car, and so we create a spell that will help them obtain one. Rather than merely praying to Deity to cause that to happen, and hope that it does, we take more direct action, and using the tools of Magick, we create a spell which causes changes in the physical world to take place, the end result of which is that our friend now has a new car.

Meditation might be used in conjunction with both spells and prayer. Meditation is the silencing or the focusing of the mind for a particular purpose. When we are listening for an answer from Deity, that is a form of meditation. We are silencing our own mind so that we can hear the mind of Deity. When we are focusing our intent while casting a spell, that is a form of meditation. Meditation takes on many forms – we encountered a mindfulness meditation back in Step 6. There are guided meditations, and there are practices such as Yoga and martial arts, which often make use of meditation.

With each of these, we are improving our conscious contact with Deity, and that is an activity that too many of us spend insufficient time practicing.. We have grown so used to having Deity in the background of our lives that we expend little energy in developing and improving that "conscious contact" with them. Conscious Contact implies that we no longer relegate Deity to the background – they are no longer an assumption, but become much more real; it becomes an integral part of our daily lives. And the relationship becomes then, much more interactive; it becomes a partnership. And when we partner with Deity, mighty and marvelous things are bound to happen – and chief among these is our the continuing maintenance of our sobriety.

In the original version of the Twelve Steps, as published by Alcoholics Anonymous the final phrase is "Praying only for knowledge of His will for us, and the power to carry that out." For the purpose of this text, we have modified it to read "praying for knowledge and understanding of our own highest will, the Divine plan for us, and the power to carry that out." As Pagans, we recognize that our partnership with Deity places us in control of our own destinies. Our ultimate destiny is not merely to have the opportunity to sit in worship of the Divine for eternity. The Pagan concept of Deity (for many Pagans) is not some being that exists outside, apart from, or withdrawn from the world, but something that is also existential, something which subsists within us as well. Deity can be immanent as well as transcendent. We don't mean to insult the Judeo-Christian-Islamic faiths with these concepts, but our view of Divinity is dramatically different than theirs.

As different as is the Pagan concept of Deity, so are the concepts of life and eternity. This life – for most Pagans – is but one of many, and the plan that we have for ourselves and for our growth involves more than a single lifetime. Our goal, when working with Deity and with our higher self, involves discerning what our own plan is for this particular lifetime. What lessons did we come here to learn? What experiences did we wish for ourselves? What agreements might we have with those who share this life with us? Paganism is not a religion of "Let it be done to me according to your will", but an active religion, in which we have already made choices, and in which our own will is particularly valuable and important.

## Step 11 Practical Application

The practical uses of Step 11 are manifold. For those of us who don't yet have an active life of worship and prayer, Step 11 is an opportunity make a beginning. For those of us who already have an active spiritual life, this is an opportunity to take our spiritual practices to a higher level. For the Neo-Pagan, this can involve experimentation with more and new ways to experience our faith. Here are some questions to ponder:

➤ How many of your spiritual path's sacred days do you recognize?
➤ Do you celebrate lunar events as well as solar events?
➤ Do you take time daily to meditate or pray?
➤ Do you perform magick?
➤ How often do you visit places that you consider sacred?
➤ Do you spend enough time reading books or watching films of a spiritual nature?
➤ How much time do you devote to listening to spiritual music?
➤ How often do you pray for others?
➤ Do you spend as much time on matters of faith as you do for your own entertainment?
➤ Do you engage in prayer or meditation prior to making big decisions?
➤ Do you engage in prayer or meditation prior to making smaller, or seemingly less important or impactful decisions?

The point of these questions is to come to an understanding of where your faith is positioned in the scheme of things within your own life. Some of the above questions might not apply to your particular spiritual tradition, but we should all know where in our lives our faith stands, and whether or not we might give it a higher priority.

When we are trying to recover from any sort of addictive or compulsive behavior, it is important to not leave a vacuum where that addiction or compulsion once held sway over our lives. Nature, it is said, abhors a vacuum, and this includes human nature. The hole that is left when we jump on the wagon will necessarily be filled with something. Early on we may fill it entirely with recovery meetings, and that is a great substitute. But in the end, we do recover so that we can live life effectively, not so that we can attend recovery meetings. This doesn't mean that we dispense with meetings – they will, for most of us, remain an important part of our lives for as long as we live. Still, the point of recovery is to live a full and effective life, and to do this, we need to make our spirituality an integral part of our sobriety. To facilitate this, we may feel a need to assess just what part our spirituality does, and will play in our lives.

To the extent our life has changed thus far by achieving sobriety, through attending Twelve Step meetings, and all that is involved in our recovery program, improving our conscious contact with Deity – devoting ourselves to a renewed experience of our personal spirituality – is often like jump-starting that sobriety with a brand-new and fully charged battery. Now that our minds have been clear for a time, we can look at our own faith and see how it can take on a new and more prominent role in our lives. Here are some ideas that we might consider:

➢ If we haven't yet trained in or studied a particular path, are we ready to do so?

➢ Can we change our behavior even more than we already have – replacing rage with a moment of prayer, for example?

➢ If we've never engaged in personal daily or seasonal ritual activities, are we ready to do so?

➢ Do we have an established sacred space in our home?

➢ If we are part of a group, might we be ready to take on more of a leadership role?

➢ If we are of sufficient learning, might we be ready to teach or to take on students?

➢ If we are solitary, can we consider working with a group at some point?

➢ Are we ready to organize a public ritual?

➢ Are we ready to work toward taking on some more responsibilities in the group we work with?

➢ Are we ready to perhaps volunteer as clergy in prisons or in a hospital?

➢ Could we organize a spiritual book or film club, meeting to discuss the titles on a regular basis?

➢ Could we organize a group of people to bring ritual to the shut-ins in our area?

➢ Are we willing to do volunteer work on behalf of our tradition? (Adopting a park or wilderness area, and keeping it clean, for example.)

Obviously not everything on this entire list will be accessible to everyone – not all of us are going to be acting as clergy or as chaplains, and not all of us are cut out to teach others. But on this list are things that we can all achieve if we set our minds to doing it. There is certainly no one among us who is doing everything they can for their faith – as humans, we are all fallible, and there is always something that we can do to improve our conscious contact with Deity on a daily basis.

The things that we can do to increase our conscious contact with deity are almost limitless. Our day-to-day lives are filled with countless opportunities to express our spirituality – and as we grow, we will become increasingly aware of them. We might recognize that Step 11 is not a one-time exercise; it is a way of life which constantly demonstrates to us ways that we can come closer to our Goddesses and Gods, and to our own higher purpose. This improved conscious contact with our Higher Powers is not something that is uniquely Pagan; it is something that has been consistently sought after by all people with a real and abiding faith in their gods.

## Step 11 Ritual

In Step 11 we place a greater level of emphasis on our spirituality than we have in the past. We are challenged to express our relationship with Deity in ways that we as yet have not, and to call forth and expect an experience with Deity that is greater and deeper than we have ever known in our spiritual practices thus far. Whatever it is that we do for Step 11, it is but a starting point. If we are truly choosing to improve our conscious contact with Goddess, with God, with the Divine as we experience it, this implies that we already have such a connection – and indeed at this point in our recovery, we should. Hopefully by this time we have recognized that some power beyond our understanding has been able to assist us in achieving something we were not able to do on their own. So we will first look squarely at our spiritual life and determine how it can be improved.

Let's look first at who we profess to be, and see if that squares with our practice. It's likely that most people reading this book are Wiccan. If so, how often do you celebrate the Sabbats? What about the Esbats? Some of us might be practitioners of Asatru or Druidry, Druidism or Strega or DCW or a follower of any of countless other traditions. How many of us have actively sought to celebrate, for just one year, each of the traditional celebrations or seasonal rituals for that year? Many of us claim to be eclectic. For those of us who are, let me ask another question: Do we claim to be eclectic because it's convenient? Do we claim eclecticism because it's too difficult to commit to a particular path? Perhaps we once sought to join a group, but working within that group's structure was a little too difficult, or it required a level of commitment that we weren't prepared to give. Step 11 calls us out of that shell of fear or of laziness that has kept us from more fully engaging with Deity. It calls us to step out of our prior comfort zone and to put our spirituality at the forefront. And so in our ritual for Step 11 we are going to commit – to the Gods and to our selves.

Our ritual begins with pen in hand. We will define our faith – whether it be Wicca, Druid, DCW, Strega, Faerie, Goddess Spirituality – whatever. To improve that contact with Deity, we must know how we are going to do so. If we've sat on the edges for too long, it's time to get away from the edges and into the center of our spirituality. This doesn't mean that if you're an eclectic, you must choose a tradition. But it does mean that as an eclectic, it's time to have some definition of what that faith consists of for you personally. In defining this, we will make a decision as to which celebrations we will definitely celebrate. It may be the eight solar festivals; it may be the thirteen full moons, it may be the Pagan interpretation of traditional cultural holidays. It may be all of these. The point is to decide right here and right now what our religious holidays are. So find a quiet place, and in a special book, write down what it means to you to practice the religion you claim as your own. What does it require of you? And then, in the presence of your Goddesses, Gods, your Higher self, as honestly as possible, decide how you can do better at insuring that you do these things. Listening to Deity, write down what comes to mind.

Next we will want to set aside some regular devotional time. For many Pagans, devotional time outside of ritual, is non-existent. We go about our days and think about the Goddesses and Gods little if at all. But all of our spiritual leaders, from whatever religious tradition they may have followed, have known and have taught that a truly spiritual life could not exist without some time spent on something of a regular basis in prayer, meditation, or other communion. When we speak of contact with anyone, this doesn't happen by merely thinking about them on occasion. Improving contact with anyone involves speaking and listening – communicating. For some of us, the idea of getting on our knees every morning or every evening is overly Christian. We want something that is different. But really, what's wrong with being on one's knees before their Goddess or God? If the Goddesses and Gods are real, is showing a modicum of humility before them wrong? This doesn't mean that it's a requirement for all of us, nor may it be appropriate for every path, but for many, a kneeling prayerful position demonstrates honest humility.

If praying on your knees just doesn't work, then perhaps something like a morning constitutional walk might. In parts of the country where the weather gets cold or rainy, this may not always be convenient, but it might work out. Or perhaps we might consider a daily Yoga, Tai Ch'i or martial art routine, or some other activity, with meditation and prayer as part of that routine. What we are trying to do is to find a way that we can have regular communication with Deity.

I took part in a panel discussion at a local university and I heard a young woman ask a man how often he meditates. His response was "Always." Our lives can truly be a meditation, a communion with Deity, but this can't happen unless we move in that direction. And so this ritual is our first step to making our entire life a prayer, an offering, a ritual dedicated to whoever our Deity is.

In the end, Step 11 isn't a one-time ritual; it doesn't end. It's not something we can do once and be done with; it's a way of life

that not only results from having practiced these Twelve Steps –
it's much, much more than that. It's a way of life that will give us
the wherewithal to continue living sober for as long as we practice
it.

# Step 12

*Having achieved a spiritual awakening as the result of these steps, we tried to carry this message to others like our selves, and to practice these principles in all our affairs.*

The theme of Step 12 is giving back. It's a spiritual principle that to keep something, we need to be willing to give it away, and this is the essence and the fundamental mystery of sobriety. It was recognized early on that an alcoholic was uniquely able to reach another alcoholic, and that principle seems to apply to any addict or compulsive person. Perhaps this is because like a wilderness guide, we who have been in that dark wilderness know the way out. Or maybe it's some sort of empathy or wisdom gained from having been in the same situation as the person we seek to help. Whatever it is, it works.

Many people who embrace the Twelve Steps have wondered when first reading them, and coming upon Step 12, just what is a spiritual awakening. Some of us might think of the Christian saint Paul who was struck with some sort of bolt from the heavens, came to know Christ, and recognized the error of his ways, repenting there and then, to become a Christian. Many others think of some sort of brilliant insight that suddenly illuminates the dark corners of their mind, enabling them all at once to see things as they were never able to before, perhaps crying out *Eureka!* They expect an epiphany, a life-changing moment, something dramatic and unexpected. But not all spiritual awakenings are of the same sort. Not everyone has a life-changing moment. Just think to the morning and how you may have awakened today. Some of us have alarm clocks – we are sleeping, they ring, and we are awake. But sometimes the power may be out, or we may not have set a clock to wake us. We are sleeping, and we gradually awaken; can we point to the moment when we were asleep, and the next when we were awake? Some awakenings are dramatic, disruptive, almost rude – others are so gentle that we barely notice them.

Likewise, a spiritual awakening doesn't have to be of any particular sort to be valid. For some, there are those brilliant moments of insight where we know or understand something deeply that we hadn't known just moments before. But arguably the most important insights we obtain are those we gain only gradually – the lessons that are hard ones, and which take a great deal of time and effort to integrate into our personalities and habits.

Two of the most profound spiritual insights are articulated in the very words of Step 12 – that we are to carry the message, and that we need to practice these principles in all of our affairs.

Perhaps what is seemingly the most difficult task at hand is to practice these principles in all our affairs. We have come to experience Twelve Steps – we admitted we were powerless over our addiction or habit; we came to believe that a power beyond us could help us find sanity; we turned our lives over to the care of that Deity which could help us; we made a searching and fearless moral inventory of our lives. We admitted to our Gods, to our selves, and to another human being the exact nature of our wrongs; we became willing to have Deity change us. We asked Deity to help us to effect that change. We then made a list of people we had harmed, became willing to make amends to them, and we made direct amends. We continued to take a personal inventory of our selves, and took responsibility then, and there, when we found our selves in error. We sought through prayer and meditation to improve our conscious contact with deity. And now we are saying that we will practice all of these principles, not just in relation to our habits or addiction or compulsion, but in *all* our affairs. Just how do we go about this?

It's important to remember one lesson that we have learned when we have worked this far through the steps – namely, that our addictions or habits or compulsions have affected every aspect of our lives, and that likely, most every facet of our lives was used at some point as an excuse or had been a trigger to whatever habit or addiction or compulsion it was that made our lives unmanageable in the first place. In the midst of our struggles, we used when times were good, or when times were bad. We used to celebrate a new love, or to drown the misery of loves lost. We used when business was good, or when we were on the verge of bankruptcy. The point is that every aspect of our life was an excuse to engage in whatever it was that ultimately became our downfall. When we make it a point to utilize everything we have learned that has led us to recovery in all aspects of our lives, in all our affairs, then we are making available that healing energy, the magick that is contained within the Twelve Steps in all of our affairs, in all aspects of our lives, and with this, we are inoculating our entire life against the conditions that might lead us to relapse.

We are also taking the tools that we have just used to build anew our character, and working with them to establish that same character in every relationship that we have. No longer is our entire life unmanageable. We are discovering that our life is not only manageable, but successful because we are acting with integrity – in how we deal with a co-worker, a business partner, another recovering addict or alcoholic. We interact with each of these people, utilizing the same principles; honesty, compassion and integrity. Some have suggested (jokingly) that this is a poor proposition for a used car salesperson, but in general there are few if any aspects of our lives that cannot be improved if we apply the principles of being honest, taking responsibility for our actions, and trusting in Deity to steer us in the right direction. And maybe that's a spiritual awakening too – that we don't actually have to go through this life, making things up as we go along – that some sense of direction is available to each of us if we are willing only to seek it out.

As Pagans, we embrace mystery – we are very familiar with apparent paradoxes, and the value of the lessons we find within them. In hearing that to keep what we have we must be willing to give it away, we find one of those mysteries. What we are to offer freely is our experience, strength and hope – our service in helping others discover and obtain sobriety. What we gain from that experience is our own renewed hope that for one more day, we will enjoy that sobriety. Among those of us who have experienced addiction and subsequent recovery, it is almost universally true that those who maintain sobriety are those who help others discover sobriety ... and that is how we are able to keep that which we give away.

## Step 12 Practical Application

We apply Step 12 in our lives when we become willing to help others, and do so. Some of us are afraid to do this – we have a fear that we'll say the wrong thing, that someone we hope will "get it" doesn't, or that they go back into addiction again. Helping others can be very daunting because it brings up memories of our own past. We fear that if they go back out that we might as well. We fear that if we work too closely with another that we might get too close to our own triggers. Perhaps our fear is that we won't be as good at helping others as were those who helped us. When we have those feelings, the truth is that we are putting our faith in the wrong things, and rather than seeking to help another we might be seeking to build up our own pride.

If our job is to help others and to carry the message to them, there are a few things to remember: First among these is this – the message isn't from us. It's a message that began with Dr. Bob and Bill W. And that message is that recovery is possible – we can end the insanity of the cycle of addiction or compulsion and attain recovery in our lives. Our job isn't to get anyone else sober – we are simply the carriers of a message that was sent out quite some time ago. That's our only job. And just as we had the opportunity to accept or reject that message, so do those to whom we carry it. It wasn't anyone else's job to get us sober – we did that work, with the help of Deity. It's not our job to get anyone else sober – that task belongs to them.

The second thing to remember is this: If someone truly wishes to embrace recovery in their life, they will. If we carry the message, and they are willing, we can't say anything wrong – they want it, and they will get it. If they do not wish to embrace that recovery, then there is nothing that we can say to convince them that we have something they might want. If they aren't ready to embrace a lifestyle of sobriety, then what we have is not yet of value to them, and nobody wishes to spend the energy and time necessary to achieve sobriety until they are ready.

So, how do we go about carrying this message? If you are active in a group, then you're already doing that! If you attend meetings, think back to that first day you walked into a room and saw another person there. You likely realized at that moment that you weren't alone. That's carrying the message. You likely saw coffee or cookies or some other snack available; those who make the coffee, set up the rooms, those who chair the meetings and have positions within the various groups are also carrying the message. Many programs have telephone hot-lines available in which people who are in the program are willing to accept calls from people looking for information as to where a meeting might be held, or how to find a ride to a meeting. Those who answer the phones are carrying the message.

Most Twelve Step programs also embrace the idea of sponsorship. A sponsor is an individual who is active in the program that is willing to make themselves available to another in their journey through these twelve steps. Think of a sponsor as a guide – they have worked their way through the wilderness, and are familiar with it, and are comfortable with the idea of leading another person safely through that wilderness. A sponsor isn't an "expert"; a sponsor is simply a person who has already been there. Most sponsors will also agree that the act of sponsorship does as much, if not more, for maintaining their own sobriety as it does for the person they are sponsoring.

We also carry the message in the way we live our day-to-day lives. In living a sober life, we become a model to others. We don't have to break our anonymity in doing so – we are simply living an effective life. And it is no mystery that when an individual has a problem, they come to those who seem to have a solution to that problem. Our children, our family members and close friends might know that we are part of such a group, and when they know of someone in need of what we have, they'll ask us if it's okay to send someone our way. Some people who have no problem with addictions or compulsive behaviors will also see there is something different about us. We might hear "How can you stay so calm?" or "Why don't you seem to get angry?" This is the evidence that the program is working in our lives.

## Step 12 Ritual

Because Step 12 is about carrying the message, the ritual for Step 12 is about just that. Remember back to Step 3, and the ritual that you did then. We discovered that we need to be able to rely on another person for help – we need to discover that we can trust. The ritual for Step 12 is the ritual for Step 3, with the exception that you are now the guide, the person assisting.

As that person you are helping over the bridge, blindfolded, accomplishes her or his task, think about their fear, and about the confidence they are obtaining. Recognize that this is a gift that you are offering to another human being. You have been granted a spiritual awakening as the result of these steps, and are now in a position to offer that same gift to another human being.

What could be more fitting?

## Appendix I: The Author's Story

When I was young, the first thing that I can remember is being uncomfortable in my own skin – I knew that somehow, I just didn't fit. And as I grew, I found that my level of discomfort did not diminish. The nature of that discomfort is unimportant – what is important is that I've met few addicts, alcoholics, people with mental illness or eating disorders who were ever truly comfortable with who they were. Somehow, everyone I've met who has suffered like me has experienced these feelings in some form or other.

I recall my family telling me that my first experience with a mind-altering substance happened when I was quite young. Parties and Sunday dinners at my grandmother's house or the homes of other relatives quite often were celebrated with wine, and at a very young age I was going about looking for sips. I remember as a young teen feeling quite nice at my uncle's bar when I was treated to a rum and Coke. In high school I would raid my parent's liquor cabinet, and one of my first prized possessions was a flask in which I could bring booze with me to school.

Throughout all this time, I had other characteristics – I was terribly impatient and impulsive. Living in a town that the railroad passed through, trains were often obstacles, and jumping on from one side and off on the other was almost a given. Hopping on a train was a neighborhood challenge, but nobody followed me the day that I ran beneath one of the chemical cars. It wasn't until years later that dealing with that sort of impulsive behavior became important in my treatment plan.

Like most kids who are uncomfortable with who they are, I found myself on the wrong side of many jokes and physical attacks while at school. I grew up understanding what it meant to be the target of bullies in an era when teachers somehow suspected that getting picked on implied that the one picked on must have somehow provoked the other. In 8th grade, the school's solution was to hold me back one year with the hope that a change of playmates might change the situation – it didn't.

During my high school years, my depression and self-loathing worsened; but I discovered that with a job and income, I could have other playmates. I was in High School, working in a now defunct shoe factory during the summer, when I was first introduced to marijuana and other substances. I absolutely loved the release that some of these substances offered. I could be completely carefree – at times the only care being how to stop laughing. At other times though, the paranoia that followed was almost unbearable.

What strikes me about those years is that the drugs and the alcohol were coping mechanisms, but they did nothing to help me deal with life in an effective manner. The temporary relief helped me mask, to myself and others, what I was feeling; in that sense, they probably helped me survive my youth. They also masked some of the symptoms of the mental illness that I was suffering. But in the end, temporary relief and permanent solutions are quite different things. I had none of the latter.

Over the years of trying to cope but never properly dealing with things, I submitted to my family's desires for me. I got involved in the church music ministry. I joined the Air Force after high school; I tried to "be the person God wanted me to be", but was unable to discover who I actually was. Eventually I married, and I do have two beautiful daughters – something I will never regret – but marriage was just another attempt at trying to be somebody for someone else.

After about 14 years of being married, after a number of jobs and continually trying to hold things together, my life started to fall apart. The marriage was already on a rocky road, and my partner was not able to deal with a person who couldn't figure out who they were, so we divorced. At this point in my life I no longer had any capacity to make things appear normal. Drugs, alcohol and mental illness had taken their toll and I went through what people used to call a nervous breakdown. I was suicidal and uncontrollable and spent the next four years in and out of mental hospitals. I was put on some fairly heavy anti-psychotics, mood stabilizers, antidepressants and other medications. All the while, I never quit using other substances. I managed to convince myself that if my problem was mental, then I didn't really have a substance abuse issue.

Sometimes the feeling of emptiness was overwhelming. People think that depression is continual sadness, but I discovered that it's much more than this – with sadness, there is a precipitating loss; it's understandable. Sadness is a grief process, a mourning, and while it's very uncomfortable, you can point to a cause and see that loss leaves a void, and while what was lost may not be replaced, that void can be filled – eventually. Depression leaves a person feeling not just sad, but empty. It is like the void of loss or sadness, but without any definable loss. There is nothing to point to, and you don't know where that void is so there is nothing to fill. Just to feel something, I began to injure myself. Somehow, physical pain was better than the nothingness of depression.

I moved from place to place, at times living in situations in which even my daughters didn't want to be with me. I found myself homeless, staying on friend's couches until they tired of me; at one point I spent a few weeks in a tent. But somehow I managed to convince myself that I was never homeless.

One day, my therapist suggested that I look at my substance use. suggesting that I might have a problem in that area. I was a bit indignant at the idea – my problems, after all, stemmed all from mental illness. Mentioning to some friends what this therapist said, one remarked "You don't have any more of a problem than I do." This particular comment made me blink because I suspected that friend actually did have a problem. Somewhat floored by that revelation, I called a hotline and decided to check out a Twelve Step meeting in my area.

At that first meeting, I was determined, not to get help, but to compare myself to each of those there. I was looking for differences, a way to prove that my problems and theirs were not the same. And I was able to do so! I heard tales of arrests for DUI or OUI, time spent in jail, lost jobs, homes, cars. They had been in prisons. They had physically assaulted people they loved. In my mind, none of this applied to me. I also heard a great deal of talk about God and of Jesus Christ, whom I wanted nothing to do with. And so after a few meetings, I was convinced that a group such as this was not for me. Until one fall day, that is.

The medications I was on could not relieve the darkness that had enveloped me. I felt useless, unwanted, unloved, unnecessary ... all the while wanting to be wanted, to have a purpose, but with no clear vision of that ever becoming possible. I thought that my daughters would actually be better off without me, and I was fairly certain that my family wouldn't really care if I was gone. I had attempted suicide a number of times before, but this time something was different. I remember going to the liquor store and purchasing a few bottles, and I had just refilled some of my medications, and sat down, drinking and taking pills. I vaguely remember getting up and starting to walk, but my next memory was of waking up in the intensive care ward in my local hospital.

Apparently, I had stumbled into a major avenue in my city at about the time one of my friends was driving by. She managed to get me into her car, but I was completely incoherent, and she took me to the hospital. I was so combative that I was put in restraints. I don't recall what was done to save my life, but I remember the indignity of having the various tubes removed. I remember the concerned and disappointed faces of my friends.

I don't know what words I said to the counselor or social worker on that day, but strangely enough, I wasn't sent to a psychiatric hospital that time. I do remember that shortly after, I logged on to an online recovery forum and talked about the experience. Someone replied and asked me "What will it take?" He said that if I only got on the wagon, he'd help push. He sounded honest, sincere, and more than that, he cared. At that point it hadn't yet hit me that I had quite nearly succeeded in killing myself. But the words this person used had brought me to tears – here was a man who didn't know me at all, and he sincerely cared what would happen to me. So, that day, I resolved to at least try to do what it would take to get well. I became convinced that there were other people at least as bad off as I was, who did recover.

As I started attending more recovery meetings, I realized that I wasn't alone, nor was I special. Where I previously had thought that smart people weren't in need of recovery, I started meeting smart people in recovery: doctors, nurses, engineers, college professors, lawyers, carpenters, plumbers, electricians, physicists, counselors, therapists, construction workers – no group of people was immune from these ills, and the Twelve Step programs worked for all of them.

When I first started attending meetings, my self-esteem was as low as it could possibly be. I didn't want to be seen, so I just sat there – never raising my hand to talk, never even going to the bathroom because I didn't want anyone to see me. I talked to few people. But slowly, I began to open my mouth and I discovered that nobody cared how low I had been – what mattered was that I was there and getting better. Still very self conscious, and afraid of rejection, I realized that these programs work better when you have a sponsor. So I found a woman whose life I admired, and I asked her one night if she might consider helping me to find a sponsor. I didn't want her to say "I can't sponsor you", so I figured this was the easy way to not feel rejection once more. She agreed to sponsor me, and has been my sponsor since.

About nine months into this, I felt it was time to work the Twelve Steps formally, and I sought out another woman whom I respect to do this with. It was in this process that I learned that I really wasn't that bad. However horrible I thought I was, my worst critic was myself, and I had punished myself far more than I deserved. I still had restitution to make, I still needed to hold myself accountable for a number of things, but these were all debts that could be paid.

It was also at about this time that I was introduced to someone who hosted a radio program on a local station, and he wanted to interview me. I agreed to that; and some time after that interview, he told me that he was getting a promotion at the station, and his program was going to end unless I took that position. I had never done radio before, but this man thought I was up to the task. I thought it might be fun and so I began the training program under his tutelage. This program changed over the years, and eventually became the program that is now PaganFM! It's amazing that just a year prior to this, I could not follow through on much of anything – I'd get frightened or insecure, and I'd quit. As of this writing, PaganFM! has aired every week for well over three years.

All during my recovery, I made a commitment to improve my relationship with my daughters. My oldest hadn't spoken to me since about my first hospitalization, but I promised myself that I would do whatever it took to be there for both of them. The first breakthrough, for me, was when my oldest was sick one day, and asked me to come over and cook some Alfredo for her. This was always one of my specialties, but my first inclination was that this wasn't cheap, I didn't have much money, and I was busy. However, this was my daughter, and she wasn't feeling well, and it was my time to step up. So I went to the store and bought everything I would need ... and cooked for my daughter. I suspect it may have been a bit of a test on her part, but I was very glad for the opportunity to pass it.

Since then our relationship has continually improved. I remember one day when I was driving her to college and I asked her straight out – "We're talking again; what changed?" She looked at me and said "You're not crazy anymore." Indeed, I had been crazy, but the steps were effecting in me a change that I could not have done on my own.

Now it's more than five years since I stepped foot in one of those rooms of recovery. I've met countless people – some who have made it, others that haven't. Some people that I grew to love in those rooms have died, succumbing to their illness, or to the challenges of life. Others have made remarkable changes in their lives, taking on challenges on with a dignity and grace that most people would find difficult to imagine.

My oldest daughter has moved about halfway across the country, but we speak at least three or four times every week. My youngest is in high school, and I am the semi-official DJ for her school at every dance. I've been at the radio station for over four years now, and my program has been heard all around the world. I've heard from many listeners that what I do each and every week has helped them live their lives more fully. Where before, I was afraid to be seen or heard, I'm now blessed to spread a message of hope.

But I have to remind myself every day that what I have is very tenuous; I could lose it just as quickly as I received it. The only thing that keeps me from relapse, from falling back into that cycle of mental illness and depression and mania and substance abuse is vigilance and honesty. I have managed to keep myself accountable to others in these rooms of recovery. I let people know how I'm feeling, what's on my mind. And they do the same with me. If I don't have to keep how I'm feeling a secret, things aren't going to build inside like some stopped up pressure cooker.

On my own I was hopeless – today I have hope. Today I have a reason to look forward to tomorrow. I realize now that I am here for a reason and I have something to contribute and I can bring beauty into this world.

No matter what your problem is – be it drugs, alcohol, mental illness, eating disorders, gambling, online gaming, smoking or anything else, there is likely a Twelve Step group that can help you out. They don't magically make your problems go away, but they can certainly help you deal with them head-on. There is no reason to live in misery or shame, no reason to have a life that's out of control and unmanageable. Someone once said that no matter how many steps you have taken to live in shame and misery, it's only twelve steps out. And Twelve steps is short enough a journey for anyone with even a modicum of willingness to begin.

## Appendix II: Twelve Step Programs

Here we provide a listing of Twelve Step Groups, a brief description of their program, and contact information for those seeking help. Inclusion of a Twelve Step program's information in this text does not imply an endorsement of that group by the author, nor does inclusion of any Twelve Step program imply their endorsement of this text.

It should also be noted that even within a given program there may be vast differences between groups or meetings. If you seek out a group, and discover that a particular meeting is unwelcoming or otherwise not to your liking, don't give up – check the meeting schedules; you may find that another group, or another meeting within the same program will be better suited to your taste, or there might be a related program in your area as well. That said, try to make sure that the reason you don't like a particular group is valid; many of us have left groups or meetings not because there was something wrong with them, but rather because of our own prejudices or defense mechanisms.

This list of Twelve Step programs is not exhaustive, and includes only some of the programs which have implemented a Twelve Step program based on those steps created by Bill W. and Dr. Bob. It does not include programs which, while based on a Twelve Step model, have not based their program on the original Twelve Steps as created by Alcoholics Anonymous.

All versions of the Twelve Steps follow a similar format – in this text we have used a generic version, adapted slightly for Pagans. The following list shows text from the original Twelve Steps of Alcoholics Anonymous, with the words that have been removed or replaced *(in italics)*, and the words that have been added **underlined**.

Step 1. We admitted that we were powerless *(over alcohol)*, and that our lives had become unmanageable.

Step 2. Came to believe that a power greater than ourselves could restore us to sanity.

Step 3. Made a decision to turn our will and our lives over to the care of *(God as we understood Him)* **the Divine and our own highest self**.

Step 4. Made a searching and fearless moral inventory of ourselves.

Step 5. Admitted to *(God)* **Deity**, to ourselves, and to another human being the exact nature of our wrongs.

Step 6. Were entirely ready *(to have God remove all these defects of character)* **to effect, with the help of Deity, a profound change in our character.**

Step 7. Humbly *(asked Him to remove our shortcomings)* **implored Deity to help us effect that change.**

Step 8. Made a list of all persons we had harmed and became willing to make amends to them all.

Step 9. Made direct amends to such people wherever possible, except when to do so would injure them or others.

Step 10. Continued to take personal inventory and when we were wrong promptly admitted it.

Step 11. Sought through prayer and meditation **and our craft** to improve our conscious contact with *(God as we understood Him)* **Deity**, *(praying only for knowledge of His will for us and the power to carry that out)* **praying for knowledge and understanding of our own highest will, the Divine plan, and the power to carry that out.**

Step 12. Having achieved a spiritual awakening as the result of these steps, we tried to carry this message to *(alcoholics)* **others like our selves**, and to practice these principles in all our affairs.

Now we take a look at a number of Twelve Step programs, some implementations of the Twelve Steps, and how to get in touch with those organizations that may be of use to us.

# Alcoholics Anonymous

Alcoholics Anonymous was the first program of recovery to utilize the Twelve Steps; every Twelve Step program that exists today traces its heritage back to these steps. Alcoholics Anonymous is a program of recovery from alcoholism, and does not offer help for any other problems. While many in recovery from other substances do attend open meetings, and while Alcoholics Anonymous recognizes that many of its members have problems other than alcoholism, AA sticks to its primary purpose – recovery from alcoholism. That may be one reason why it has survived and thrived.

Alcoholics Anonymous charges no dues or fees for membership and are fully self-supporting through voluntary contributions by their members.

## Contacting Alcoholics Anonymous

Alcoholics Anonymous is listed in virtually every telephone book in the United States, and in many throughout the world. Most have a toll-free hotline that will get you in touch with someone who can tell you where a meeting is taking place, and often arrange for transportation.

Their number is usually located in the business section of your phone book (often an 800 number).

Website: http://www.aa.org
Alcoholics Anonymous operates a multi-lingual website which has a meeting locator function, allowing you to find meetings in the U.S. and Canada. The Big Book (Alcoholics Anonymous) and the Twelve and Twelve (Twelve Steps and Twelve Traditions), which are the two texts most often used in AA meetings are both available online at this site.

There are online meetings of Alcoholics Anonymous in many languages, and the Online Intergroup can be found at:
http://aa-intergroup.org

A.A. World Services, Inc.,
P.O. Box 459,
New York, NY 10163
(212) 870-3400

## Al-Anon/Alateen

Al-Anon/Alateen is a group for people who have a family member that is a problem drinker. They recognize that to help the problem drinker, family members need help themselves first, because they have been affected by that drinking. Al-Anon/Alateen maintains a multi-lingual web site. Meetings are available world-wide, online, and by telephone.

Meeting Information: 1-888-4AL-ANON (1-888-425-2666)
Monday thru Friday, 8 am – 6 pm EST. For US and Canada.

http://www.al-anon.alateen.org
wso@al-anon.org

Al-Anon Family Group Headquarters, Inc.
1600 Corporate Landing Parkway
Virginia Beach, VA 23454-5617
Office Telephone: (757) 563-1600

## Cocaine Anonymous

Cocaine Anonymous is a Twelve Step program that helps men and women recover from addiction to Cocaine and other mind-altering substances. They provide face-to-face meetings around the world.

International Referral Line: 1-800-347-8998.

http://www.ca.org
cawso@ca.org

CAWSO (C.A. World Service Office)
21720 S. Wilmington Ave., Ste. 304
Long Beach, CA 90810-1641

## Crystal Meth Anonymous

Crystal Meth Anonymous is a Twelve Step program that helps men and women to recover from addiction to Crystal Meth. Meetings held throughout the US.

Hotline: 213-488-4455

http://www.crystalmeth.org

CMA General Services
4470 W Sunset Blvd Ste 107 PMB 555
Los Angeles, CA 90027-6302

## Debtors Anonymous

Debtors Anonymous is a Twelve Step program for those who have a desire to stop incurring unsecured debt. Debtors Anonymous holds meeting both in the United States and around the world. Telephone and online groups are also available.

Phone: 800-421-2383 / 781-453-2743

http://www.debtorsanonymous.org/
new@debtorsanonymous.org

Debtors Anonymous
General Service Office
PO Box 920888
Needham, MA 02492-0009

## COSA (Codependents of Sex Addicts)

COSA is a 12-Step recovery program for people whose lives have been impacted by the compulsive sexual behavior of others.

Phone: 866-899-COSA (2672)

http://www.cosa-recovery.org
info@cosa-recovery.org

ISO of COSA
PO Box 79908
Houston, TX 77279-9908

## Emotions Anonymous

Emotions Anonymous is a Twelve Step program for people who are seeking recovery from a variety of emotional difficulties. In their literature they claim to offer support for people dealing with "depression, anger, broken or strained relationships, grief, anxiety, low self-esteem, panic, abnormal fears, resentment, jealousy, guilt, despair, fatigue, tension, boredom, loneliness, withdrawal, obsessive and negative thinking, worry, compulsive behavior and a variety of other emotional issues." Emotions Anonymous has meetings world-wide, as well as telephone and on-line meetings. Their web site is available in multiple languages.

Office: 651-647-9712

http://www.emotionsanonymous.org/
infodf3498fjsd@emotionsanonymous.org

Emotions Anonymous International
PO Box 4245
St. Paul MN 55104-0245

# Families Anonymous

Families Anonymous is an organization for those whose lives have been touched by another's use of drugs or alcohol, or by related behavioral problems. Meetings are available in many states in the United States, and in a number of countries around the world.

Phone: 800-815-9682

http://www.familiesanonymous.org
famanon@FamiliesAnonymous.org

Families Anonymous, Inc.
P.O. Box 3475
Culver City, CA 90231-3475

# Food Addicts In Recovery Anonymous

The Food Addicts in Recovery Anonymous is an international fellowship of men and women who have experienced difficulties in life as a result of the way we eat. We joined FA either because we could not control our eating or because we were obsessed with food. Some of us have been obese, while others have been too thin or have joined because of struggles with bulimia. There are also members who have managed to stay at a normal weight but remain constantly obsessed with food and with maintaining their weight. What we have in common is that our obsession with food has kept us from living a fulfilling life.

Office: 781-932-6300

http://www.foodaddicts.org
office@foodaddicts.org

WSI Office
400 W. Cummings Park, Suite 1700
Woburn, MA 01801

## Gamblers Anonymous

Gamblers Anonymous is a Twelve Step program that helps men and women recover from a problem with gambling.

Phone: 213-386-8789

http://www.gamblersanonymous.org/
isomain@gamblersanonymous.org.

Gamblers Anonymous
International Service Office
P.O. Box 17173 Los Angeles, CA 90017

## Narcotics Anonymous

Narcotics Anonymous is a Twelve Step group for those who find themselves addicted to any type of drug. Narcotics Anonymous does not focus on the drug involved, but rather on addiction. For that reason, one will find addicts of all sorts at an NA meeting. Narcotics Anonymous groups in various areas operate local telephone hot lines that can be found in your local telephone directory under Narcotics Anonymous.

US Office: 818-773-9999
European Office: 32-2-646-6012

http://www.na.org
fsmail@na.org

NA Main Office
PO Box 9999
Van Nuys, California 91409

WSO-Europe
48 Rue de l'Été/Zomerstraat
B-1050 Brussels, Belgium

# OLGA – OLG-Anon

Online Gamers Anonymous is a Twelve Step program for those who find that they can no longer control the amount of time spent playing computer or console games of any type. OLG-Anon provides services for those who have been influenced by those addicted. OLGA has published two versions of their Twelve Steps – one for those who believe in a higher power, and another for Atheists & Agnostics. Many meetings are held online, and others are held face-to-face in various parts of the United States.

OLGA / OLG-Anon Hotline: (612)-245-1115

http://www.olganon.org

OLGA World Services
104 Miller Lane
Harrisburg, PA 17110
olga@olganon.org

## Overeaters Anonymous

Overeaters Anonymous is a Twelve Step group for people seeking recovery for food-related issues. While the majority describe their problems as being compulsive eating or overeating, some members have problems with Bulemia, Anorexia or other issues with food.

OA Information: 505-891-2664

http://www.oa.org
info@oa.org

PO Box 44020
Rio Rancho, New Mexico 87174-4020

## Pills Anonymous

Pills Anonymous is a Twelve Step program for those who recognize that they have a problem with pills. No distinction is made as to the type of pill, legally acquired or otherwise, prescription or non, pain, sleep or anything else. The only requirement for membership is a desire to stop using pills.

http://www.pillsanonymous.org
info@pillsanonymous.org

PA World Service
1849 E Guadalupe Rd
Suite C-101-133
Tempe, Arizona 85283

## Sexaholics Anonymous

Sexaholics Anonymous is a group for those who feel that they have lost control of their sexual urges, and for whom lust has become an addiction.

Phone: 615-370-6062
Toll-free: 866-424-8777

http://www.sa.org
saico@sa.org

SAICO
PO Box 3565
Brentwood, TN 37024

## Self-Mutilators Anonymous

Self-Mutilators Anonymous is a Twelve Step program for men and women who have a desire to recover from physical self-mutilation. Self mutilation is defined as injuring the body without the intent of ending one's life, and may include cutting, picking skin, scratching until blood is drawn, re-opening wounds, tearing out hair, banging one's head, swallowing objects, or any other activity that results in physical damage that is not intended to cause death.

http://selfmutilatorsanonymous.org/
info@selfmutilatorsanonymous.org

## Social Phobics Anonymous

Social Phobics Anonymous/Social Anxiety Anonymous are a group that help sufferers overcome Social Anxiety Disorder, Social phobias, shyness, Avoidant Personality Disorder and other social anxiety disorders. They have meetings in various locations in the US, and scheduled telephone meetings.

Office: (208) 473-2465
http://healsocialanxiety.com

## Pagans In Recovery

This is the only group that I was able to find online that speaks specifically to Pagans seeking recovery. It is a forum-based web site, and seems to have been in existence since about 2008. It is an active site, with online meetings available to members.

http://www.pagansinrecovery.com.

## Bibliography

**Alcoholics Anonymous** Published by Alcoholics Anonymous World Service. ISBN: 1893007162 4th Ed.

This book is the basic text of Alcoholics Anonymous. It details the program of recovery as outlined by Bill W and Dr. Bob. As well as describing the program, the text contains numerous personal stories to which readers may relate. This text is available in numerous languages.

**Overeaters Anonymous** Published by Overeaters Anonymous Inc. ISBN: 0-9609898-1-1

This is the basic text of Overeaters Anonymous, a Twelve Step group that works with people who experience compulsive behaviors in their relationship with food.

**The Jaguar That Roams the Mind.** Robert Tindall, published by Park Street Press. ISBN: 9781594772542

This is an amazing tale of one man's journey to the Amazon rain forest and his personal and spiritual adventures with Amazonian Shamanism. While not directly related to Twelve Step programs, included in this book are some amazing tales of recovery from addiction, as well as theories regarding the cause of addiction and its treatment.

**The Recovery Spiral**. Cynthia Jane Collins, M.Div. Citadel Press. ISBN: 0-8086-2512-6

The Recovery Spiral is a book about recovery using a somewhat Wiccan and Tarot approach, as well as the Twelve Steps. It includes a number of personal accounts, and a number of pagan groups have adopted this text for study and meetings.

**Twelve Steps and Twelve Traditions** Published by Alcoholics Anonymous World Service. ISBN 0-916856-01-1

Twelve Steps and Twelve Traditions describes, in detail, each of the Twelve Steps and Twelve Traditions of Alcoholics Anonymous. While the Twelve Traditions apply to the AA group, the Twelve Steps describe the program of recovery for the alcoholic in AA.

## Contacting the Author

The author is available for workshops and events. She maintains an office at One Washington Center in Dover, NH and can be reached by mail at:

Deirdre Hebert
1 Washington St. Suite 3110
Dover, NH 03820

dee@paganfm.com
1-603-617-4797

CPSIA information can be obtained
at www.ICGtesting.com
Printed in the USA
LVHW101136180723
752742LV00001B/116